NE능률 영어교과서

대한민국 고등학생 **10**명 중
4.7 명이 보는 교과서

영어 고등 교과서 점유율 1위
(7차, 2007 개정, 2009 개정, 2015 개정)

KB124662

리딩튜터

그동안 판매된
리딩튜터 1,900만 부
차곡차곡 쌓으면 19만 미터

에베레스트
21 배 높이

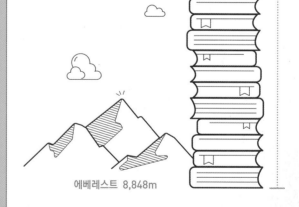

190,000m

에베레스트 8,848m

능률보카

그동안 판매된
능률VOCA 1,100만 부

대한민국 박스오피스
천만명을 넘은 영화
단 28개

VOCA

그래머존

그동안 판매된 450만 부의 그래머존을 바닥에 쭉 ~ 깔면
1000km 서울 - 부산 왕복가능

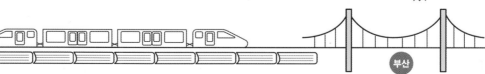

서울

부산

교재 검토에 도움을 주신 선생님들

1316
GRAMMAR LEVEL 1

지은이	NE능률 영어교육연구소
선임연구원	김지현
연구원	장경아, 가민아, 오보은
영문교열	Angela Lan
디자인	닷츠
내지 일러스트	김기환
맥편집	한서기획

Let's grow together

NE능률이
미래를
창조합니다.

건강한 배움의 고객가치를 제공하겠다는 꿈을 실현하기 위해
40년이 넘는 시간 동안 열심히 달려왔습니다.

앞으로도 끊임없는 연구와 노력을 통해
당연한 것을 멈추지 않고

고객, 기업, 직원 모두가 함께 성장하는 NE능률이 되겠습니다.

기초부터 내신까지 중학 영문법 완성

1316

1316 GRAMMAR

LEVEL
1

STRUCTURE & FEATURES

Grammar Points

최신 개정 교육과정을 분석하여 필수 문법 사항을 쉽고 명확하게 설명하였습니다.

Tip 주의! : 예외 또는 주의가 필요한 문법 사항

Tip 비교! : 비교해서 알아 두면 도움이 되는 문법 사항

✓ Grammar UP : 심화 문법 사항

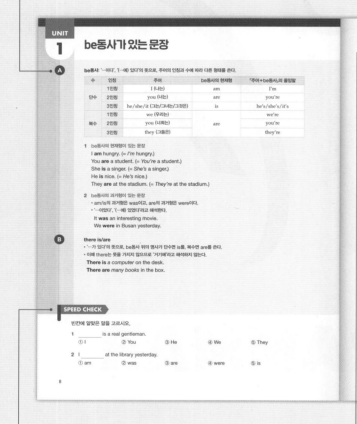

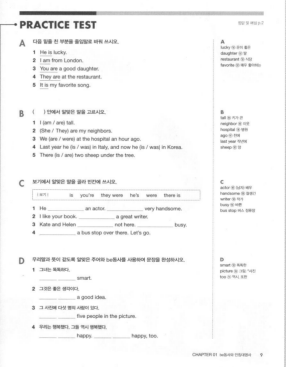

Speed Check

간단한 문제를 통해 Grammar Points에서 배운 내용을 이해했는지 확인할 수 있습니다.

Practice Test

Grammar Points에서 배운 내용을 다양한 유형의 주관식 문제를 통해 익힐 수 있습니다.

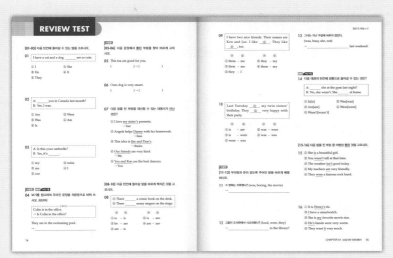

Review Test

학교 내신 시험과 가장 유사한 유형의 문제로 구성하여 실전에 대비할 수 있게 하였습니다.

NEW **내신 기출** : 최근 학교 내신에서 출제되고 있는 최신 유형

서술형 및 **고난도** : 서술형 주관식 문제 및 고난도 문제를 골고루 수록

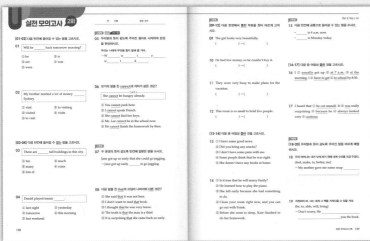

실전 모의고사

출제 확률이 높은 내신형 문제로 구성된 실전 모의고사 2회를 수록하여 실제 내신 시험을 치르는 것처럼 연습할 수 있게 하였습니다.

Workbook

서술형 주관식 문제로 구성된 Unit별 연습 문제로, 모든 문법 사항을 충분히 연습할 수 있게 하였습니다.

CONTENTS

CHAPTER

01

be동사와
인칭대명사

be동사가 있는 문장

A

be동사: '…이다', '(…에) 있다'의 뜻으로, 주어의 인칭과 수에 따라 다른 형태를 쓴다.

수	인칭	주어	be동사의 현재형	『주어＋be동사』의 줄임말
단수	1인칭	I (나는)	am	I'm
	2인칭	you (너는)	are	you're
	3인칭	he/she/it (그는/그녀는/그것은)	is	he's/she's/it's
복수	1인칭	we (우리는)	are	we're
	2인칭	you (너희는)		you're
	3인칭	they (그들은)		they're

1 be동사의 현재형이 있는 문장

I **am** hungry. (= *I'm* hungry.)

You **are** a student. (= *You're* a student.)

She **is** a singer. (= *She's* a singer.)

He **is** nice. (= *He's* nice.)

They **are** at the stadium. (= *They're* at the stadium.)

2 be동사의 과거형이 있는 문장

• am/is의 과거형은 was이고, are의 과거형은 were이다.

• '…이었다', '(…에) 있었다'라고 해석한다.

It **was** an interesting movie.

We **were** in Busan yesterday.

B

there is/are

• '…가 있다'의 뜻으로, be동사 뒤의 명사가 단수면 is를, 복수면 are를 쓴다.

• 이때 there는 뜻을 가지지 않으므로 '거기에'라고 해석하지 않는다.

There is *a computer* on the desk.

There are *many books* in the box.

SPEED CHECK

빈칸에 알맞은 말을 고르시오.

1 _____ is a real gentleman.

① I   ② You   ③ He   ④ We   ⑤ They

2 I _____ at the library yesterday.

① am   ② was   ③ are   ④ were   ⑤ is

PRACTICE TEST

정답 및 해설 p.2

A 다음 밑줄 친 부분을 줄임말로 바꿔 쓰시오.

1 <u>He is</u> lucky.
2 <u>I am</u> from London.
3 <u>You are</u> a good daughter.
4 <u>They are</u> at the restaurant.
5 <u>It is</u> my favorite song.

A
lucky (형) 운이 좋은
daughter (명) 딸
restaurant (명) 식당
favorite (형) 매우 좋아하는

B ( ) 안에서 알맞은 말을 고르시오.

1 I (am / are) tall.
2 (She / They) are my neighbors.
3 We (are / were) at the hospital an hour ago.
4 Last year he (is / was) in Italy, and now he (is / was) in Korea.
5 There (is / are) two sheep under the tree.

B
tall (형) 키가 큰
neighbor (명) 이웃
hospital (명) 병원
ago (부) 전에
last year 작년에
sheep (명) 양

C 보기에서 알맞은 말을 골라 빈칸에 쓰시오.

| 보기 | is   you're   they were   he's   were   there is |

1 He _____ an actor. _____ very handsome.
2 I like your book. _____ a great writer.
3 Kate and Helen _____ not here. _____ busy.
4 _____ a bus stop over there. Let's go.

C
actor (명) (남자) 배우
handsome (형) 잘생긴
writer (명) 작가
busy (형) 바쁜
bus stop 버스 정류장

D 우리말과 뜻이 같도록 알맞은 주어와 be동사를 사용하여 문장을 완성하시오.

1 그녀는 똑똑하다.

_____ _____ smart.

2 그것은 좋은 생각이다.

_____ _____ a good idea.

3 그 사진에 다섯 명의 사람이 있다.

_____ _____ five people in the picture.

4 우리는 행복했다. 그들 역시 행복했다.

_____ _____ happy. _____ _____ happy, too.

D
smart (형) 똑똑한
picture (명) 그림; *사진
too (부) 역시, 또한

be동사가 있는 부정문과 의문문

A

be동사가 있는 부정문: '…이 아니다', '(…에) 없다'의 뜻으로, 『be동사+not』의 형태이다.

주어	be동사+not	현재형의 줄임말		과거형의 줄임말
I	am/was not	I'm not	—	I wasn't
you	are/were not	you're not	you aren't	you weren't
he/she/it	is/was not	he's/she's/it's not	he/she/it isn't	he/she/it wasn't
we/you/they	are/were not	we're/you're/they're not	we/you/they aren't	we/you/they weren't

I**'m not** an actor. I'm a director.
Mia **isn't** in the kitchen. She's in her room.
I was in the classroom. I **wasn't** sick.

B

be동사가 있는 의문문

1 be동사가 현재형일 때: '…입니까?', '(…에) 있습니까?'의 뜻으로, 『be동사의 현재형+주어 …?』의 형태이다.

be동사+주어 …?	긍정 대답	부정 대답
Am I …?	Yes, you are.	No, you're not.
Are you …?	Yes, I am.	No, I'm not.
Is he/she/it …?	Yes, he/she/it is.	No, he/she/it isn't.
Are we …?	Yes, you/we are.	No, you're not. No, we aren't.
Are you …?	Yes, we are.	No, we aren't.
Are they …?	Yes, they are.	No, they aren't.

Am I late? – **No, you're not[you are not].**
Is she brave? – **Yes, she is.**

> **Tip 주의!** 긍정 대답인 경우 주어와 be동사를 줄여 쓰지 않는다.
> Are you sleepy? – Yes, I am. (← Yes, I'm.)

2 be동사가 과거형일 때: '…이었습니까?', '(…에) 있었습니까?'의 뜻으로, 『be동사의 과거형+주어 …?』의 형태이다.
Was he at the beach? – **Yes, he was. / No, he wasn't[was not].**
Were you happy last Christmas? – **Yes, we were. / No, we weren't[were not].**

SPEED CHECK

빈칸에 알맞은 말을 고르시오.

1 We _____ in the same grade.

① isn't   ② aren't   ③ am not   ④ be not   ⑤ not are

2 _____ it her phone number?

① Am   ② Are   ③ Is   ④ Be   ⑤ Were

PRACTICE TEST

정답 및 해설 p.2

A 다음 질문에 알맞은 대답을 쓰시오. (단, 부정문은 줄임말을 쓸 것)

1 Are you from Spain? – No, _____ _____.

2 Were they really angry? – No, _____ _____.

3 Is your book on the desk? – Yes, _____ _____.

4 Are you and Susan free tonight? – Yes, _____ _____.

A
really (부) 진짜로
angry (형) 화난
free (형) 한가한
tonight (부) 오늘 밤에

B 다음 문장을 ( ) 안의 형태로 바꿔 쓰시오. (단, 부정문은 줄임말을 쓸 것)

1 She is my sister. (부정문)

→ _____

2 You are a member of a science club. (의문문)

→ _____

3 We were tired this morning. (부정문)

→ _____

4 Nick was here yesterday. (의문문)

→ _____

5 They were at a concert last Sunday. (의문문)

→ _____

B
member (명) 회원
science club
과학 동아리
tired (형) 피곤한
concert (명) 콘서트, 음악회

C 우리말과 뜻이 같도록 be동사를 사용하여 문장을 완성하시오.

1 그녀의 머리는 길지 않다.

Her hair _____ _____ long.

2 그는 축구선수가 아니었다.

_____ _____ _____ a soccer player.

3 그녀는 어제 또 늦었니?

_____ _____ late again yesterday?

4 너는 Eric과 함께 있었니?

_____ _____ with Eric?

5 김 선생님과 이 선생님은 나의 선생님이 아니었다.

Mr. Kim and Mr. Lee _____ _____ my teachers.

C
long (형) (길이가) 긴
soccer player 축구선수
again (부) 다시, 또

인칭대명사

- 대명사는 명사를 대신하여 쓰는 말로, 인칭대명사는 사람이나 사물을 대신한다.
- 인칭에는 1인칭, 2인칭, 3인칭이 있으며, 문장에서의 역할에 따라 주격, 소유격, 목적격으로 나뉜다.

수	인칭	주격	소유격	목적격	소유대명사
단수	1인칭	I	my	me	mine
	2인칭	you	your	you	yours
	3인칭	he	his	him	his
		she	her	her	hers
		it	its	it	—
복수	1인칭	we	our	us	ours
	2인칭	you	your	you	yours
	3인칭	they	their	them	theirs

1 주격: '…은[는]', '…이[가]'의 뜻으로, 주어로 쓰인다.

She is cute. **I** like her.

They are great dancers.

2 소유격: '…의'의 뜻으로, 소유 관계를 표시하며 명사 앞에 쓴다.

He is **my** *best friend*. **His** *name* is Thomas.

3 목적격: '…을[를]'의 뜻으로, 목적어로 쓰인다.

My parents love **me**.

People eat **them** for breakfast.

4 소유대명사: '…의 것'의 뜻으로, 『소유격＋명사』를 나타낸다.

This ring is **his**. (his ← his ring)

Is this her book? – No, it's not. It's **mine**. (mine ← my book)

> **Tip 비교!** 고유명사의 격
> - 주격과 목적격: 고유명사를 그대로 사용한다.
>   **Sarah** is pretty.
>   I love **New York**.
> - 소유격과 소유대명사: 고유명사에 –'s를 붙여 사용한다.
>   It is **Amy's** dress.
>   The bicycle is **Mike's**.

SPEED CHECK

빈칸에 알맞은 말을 고르시오.

This is _____ dog, Bernard.

① ours   ② mine   ③ me   ④ my   ⑤ I

PRACTICE TEST

정답 및 해설 p.3

A a:b와 c:d의 관계가 같도록 빈칸에 알맞은 말을 쓰시오.

	a	:	b	c	:	d
1	my		mine	her		_____
2	they		their	_____		our
3	it		_____	us		our
4	he		him	you		_____
5	your		yours	his		_____
6	Sam		_____	Mary		Mary's

B ( ) 안에서 알맞은 말을 고르시오.

1 Is this pen (you / yours)?

2 This is (she / her) computer, not (his / him).

3 (I / Me) know them very well. They know (I / me), too.

4 It is (my / mine) pet. I love (it / its) very much.

B
know ⑧ 알다
well ⑨ 잘
pet ⑲ 애완동물

C 우리말과 뜻이 같도록 주어진 말을 알맞게 변형하여 빈칸에 쓰시오.

1 나는 그에게 매일 전화한다. (he)

I call _____ every day.

2 이것은 네 스마트폰이니? (you)

Is this _____ smartphone?

3 이 귀여운 신발은 그녀의 것이다. (she)

These cute shoes are _____.

4 그들의 학교는 그녀의 집 근처에 있다. (they, she)

_____ school is near _____ house.

C
call ⑧ 전화하다
every day 매일
smartphone ⑲ 스마트폰
near ㉗ …의 가까이(에)

D 우리말과 뜻이 같도록 주어진 말을 바르게 배열하시오.

1 Paul and Jane은 우리의 사촌들이다. (our, are, cousins)

Paul and Jane _____.

2 우리는 그들을 매달 방문한다. (visit, we, them)

_____ every month.

3 그 교과서는 내 것이다. (the textbook, mine, is)

_____.

D
cousin ⑲ 사촌
visit ⑧ 방문하다
textbook ⑲ 교과서

REVIEW TEST

[01-03] 다음 빈칸에 들어갈 수 있는 말을 고르시오.

01

> I have a cat and a dog. _____ are so cute.

① I　　　　　　② She
③ He　　　　　④ It
⑤ They

02

> A: _____ you in Canada last month?
> B: Yes, I was.

① Are　　　　　② Were
③ Was　　　　　④ Am
⑤ Is

03

> A: Is this your umbrella?
> B: Yes, it's _____.

① my　　　　　② mine
③ me　　　　　④ I
⑤ our

서술형　NEW　내신 기출

04 보기를 참고하여 주어진 문장을 의문문으로 바꿔 쓰시오. (6단어)

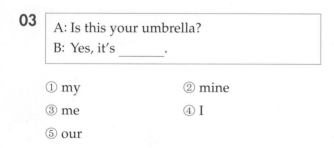

─── | 보기 | ───
Colin is in the office.
→ Is Colin in the office?

They are in the swimming pool.

→ _____

서술형

[05-06] 다음 문장에서 틀린 부분을 찾아 바르게 고치시오.

05 This tea are good for you.
(　　　　　) → (　　　　　)

06 Ours dog is very smart.
(　　　　　) → (　　　　　)

07 다음 밑줄 친 부분을 대신할 수 있는 대명사가 <u>아닌</u> 것은?

① I love <u>my sister's</u> presents.
　　　→ her
② Angela helps <u>Danny</u> with his homework.
　　　→ him
③ This idea is <u>Jim and Pam's</u>.
　　　→ theirs
④ <u>Our friends</u> are very kind.
　　　→ We
⑤ <u>You and Ron</u> are the best dancers.
　　　→ You

[08-10] 다음 빈칸에 들어갈 말을 바르게 짝지은 것을 고르시오.

08

> ⓐ There _____ a comic book on the desk.
> ⓑ There _____ many singers on the stage.

　　ⓐ　　ⓑ　　　　　　　ⓐ　　ⓑ
① is － is　　　　② is － are
③ be － are　　　④ are － are
⑤ are － is

09

I have two nice friends. Their names are Ken and Joe. I like ___ⓐ___ . They like ___ⓑ___ , too.

	ⓐ	ⓑ		ⓐ	ⓑ
①	them	– me	②	they	– my
③	their	– me	④	them	– my
⑤	they	– I			

10

Last Tuesday ___ⓐ___ my twin sisters' birthday. They ___ⓑ___ very happy with their party.

	ⓐ	ⓑ		ⓐ	ⓑ
①	is	– are	②	was	– were
③	is	– were	④	was	– was
⑤	were	– was			

서술형

[11-13] 우리말과 뜻이 같도록 주어진 말을 바르게 배열하시오.

11 그 영화는 지루했니? (was, boring, the movie)

→ _____

12 그들이 도서관에서 시끄러웠니? (loud, were, they)

→ _____ in the library?

13 그녀는 지난 주말에 바쁘지 않았다.

(was, busy, she, not)

→ _____ last weekend.

NEW 내신 기출

14 다음 대화의 빈칸에 공통으로 들어갈 수 있는 것은?

A: _____ she at the gym last night?
B: No, she wasn't. She _____ at home.

① Is[is] ② Was[was]
③ Are[are] ④ Were[were]
⑤ Wasn't[wasn't]

[15-16] 다음 밑줄 친 부분 중 어법상 틀린 것을 고르시오.

15 ① She is a beautiful girl.
② You wasn't tall at that time.
③ The weather isn't good today.
④ My teachers are very friendly.
⑤ They were a famous rock band.

16 ① It is Henry's tie.
② I have a smartwatch.
③ She is my favorite movie star.
④ He's hands were very warm.
⑤ They want it very much.

17 B에 들어갈 대답으로 알맞은 것은?

> A: Were they in San Francisco last week?
> B: _____

① Yes, they was.　② No, they were.

③ No, they weren't.　④ Yes, they weren't.

⑤ No, they wasn't.

고난도

18 다음 대화 중 자연스럽지 <u>않은</u> 것은?

① A: Excuse me. Are you Sally?

　B: Yes, I am.

② A: Mr. Jackson, am I in your class?

　B: Yes, I am.

③ A: Is this for your sister?

　B: No, it isn't. It's for my mom.

④ A: Was Nicole a singer?

　B: No, she wasn't.

⑤ A: Are Michael and Danny brothers?

　B: No, they're not. They're friends.

서술형

[19-20] 우리말과 뜻이 같도록 인칭대명사와 주어진 말을 사용하여 문장을 완성하시오.

19 이것은 그의 재킷이 아니다. 그것은 내 것이다. (jacket)

　→ This is not _____ _____. It is _____.

20 그 사과파이는 아주 맛있다. 나는 그것의 냄새를 정말 좋아한다. (smell)

　→ The apple pie is delicious. I love _____
　_____.

21 다음 밑줄 친 부분의 쓰임이 나머지와 <u>다른</u> 것은?

① This watch is not <u>his</u>.

② Pizza is <u>his</u> favorite food.

③ <u>His</u> girlfriend is very funny.

④ England is <u>his</u> home country.

⑤ There are four people in <u>his</u> family.

서술형

[22-23] 인칭대명사나 be동사를 사용하여 문맥에 맞게 문장을 완성하시오.

22 This is my sister. _____ name is Ellie. _____ is kind and active. I love _____ very much.

23 A: _____ you happy yesterday?

　B: No, I _____. I _____ sad.

고난도

24 다음 중 어법상 옳은 것은 모두 몇 개인가?

> ⓐ Is Brian nice to you?
> ⓑ Are you Mike friend?
> ⓒ There is only one exit.
> ⓓ We was angry at that time.
> ⓔ They weren't at the park yesterday.

① 1개　② 2개　③ 3개

④ 4개　⑤ 5개

CHAPTER

02

일반동사

일반동사의 의미와 형태

A

일반동사: be동사나 조동사가 아닌 동사로, 주어의 동작이나 상태를 나타낸다.

be동사	be(am, are, is, was, were)
조동사	will, can, may, must, should 등
일반동사	have, love, know, feel, dance, speak, need, want 등

B

일반동사의 현재형

 현재시계는 현재의 습관이나 지속적인 상태를 나타낸다.

1 일반동사의 현재형

1) 주어가 1인칭일 때

I **want** a new bicycle.

We **need** your help.

2) 주어가 2인칭일 때

You **have** a nice car.

3) 주어가 3인칭일 때

He/She **knows** the answer.

They **run** every morning.

2 주어가 3인칭 단수일 때 일반동사의 현재형 만드는 법

규칙 변화	대부분의 동사	동사원형+-s	comes, eats, meets, sees, makes, speaks, wants, plays, runs, reads, likes, loves 등
	-o, -s, -ch, -sh, -x로 끝나는 동사	동사원형+-es	goes, does, passes, catches, teaches, watches, washes, brushes, fixes 등
	'자음+-y'로 끝나는 동사	y를 i로 고치고+-es	fly → flies, study → studies, cry → cries, try → tries, worry → worries 등
불규칙 변화	have → **has**		

My dad **loves** comedy shows.

Jason **does** his homework after dinner.

Zoey always **tries** her best.

She **has** brown hair.

SPEED CHECK

( ) 안에서 알맞은 말을 고르시오.

1 She (take / takes) a walk in the park.

2 They (know / knows) my email address.

3 Sean and Jin (go / goes) home together every day.

PRACTICE TEST

정답 및 해설 p.4

A 주어진 동사를 알맞게 변형하여 빈칸에 쓰시오. (단, 현재형으로 쓸 것)

1 You _____ beautiful eyes. (have)

2 Andy _____ on the Internet every night. (chat)

3 Mr. Brown _____ math at a high school. (teach)

4 Marie _____ her hair every morning. (brush)

5 Kathy _____ to school by subway. (go)

6 Mark and I _____ magazines together. (read)

7 She _____ mangoes for dessert. (want)

A
chat ⑧ 이야기하다
math ⑲ 수학
subway ⑲ 지하철
magazine ⑲ 잡지
dessert ⑲ 디저트, 후식

B 보기에서 알맞은 말을 골라 현재시제의 문장을 완성하시오.

| 보기 | play   cry   go   watch   pass   worry   read

1 Lily _____ every exam.

2 The baby _____ all the time.

3 Nelly _____ about her future.

4 They _____ camping on holiday.

5 I _____ with my friends after school.

6 He _____ the sitcom every Tuesday.

7 My mom _____ the newspaper in the morning.

B
all the time 항상, 줄곧
future ⑲ 미래
camping ⑲ 캠핑, 야영
holiday ⑲ 휴일, 휴가
sitcom ⑲ 시트콤
newspaper ⑲ 신문

C 우리말과 뜻이 같도록 주어진 말을 사용하여 문장을 완성하시오.

1 너는 아름답게 춤을 추는구나. (dance)
_____ _____ beautifully.

2 Tom은 새 축구화를 원한다. (want)
_____ _____ new soccer shoes.

3 우리는 일요일마다 아버지의 차를 세차한다. (wash)
_____ _____ my dad's car on Sundays.

4 그들은 컴퓨터를 잘 고친다. (fix)
_____ _____ the computer well.

5 Ted는 겨울마다 감기에 걸린다. (catch a cold)
_____ _____ _____ _____ every winter.

C
beautifully ⑪ 아름답게
catch a cold
감기에 걸리다

일반동사의 과거형

A

일반동사의 과거형

Tip 주의! 과거시제는 과거에 일어난 일이나 과거의 상태를 나타낸다.

1 규칙 변화

대부분의 동사	동사원형+-ed	want-want**ed**, talk-talk**ed**, look-look**ed**, stay-stay**ed**, enjoy-enjoy**ed** 등
'자음+-e'로 끝나는 동사	동사원형+-d	like-lik**ed**, live-liv**ed**, love-lov**ed** 등
'자음+-y'로 끝나는 동사	y를 i로 고치고+-ed	study-stud**ied**, hurry-hurr**ied**, try-tr**ied** 등
'단모음+단자음'으로 끝나는 동사	자음을 한 번 더 쓰고+-ed	stop-stop**ped**, plan-plan**ned**, chat-chat**ted**, drop-drop**ped**, step-step**ped** 등

I **looked** at the child and **smiled**.
He **studied** in the library yesterday.
The train **stopped** at the station.
The police **stepped** into the room carefully.

2 불규칙 변화

현재형과 과거형이 같은 동사	put-**put**, cut-**cut**, set-**set**, hit-**hit**, hurt-**hurt**, read-**read**, shut-**shut** 등
현재형과 과거형이 다른 동사	do-**did**, go-**went**, have-**had**, make-**made**, eat-**ate**, see-**saw**, come-**came**, meet-**met**, buy-**bought**, bring-**brought**, take-**took**, lose-**lost**, teach-**taught**, wear-**wore**, break-**broke**, give-**gave**, write-**wrote**, sleep-**slept**, drink-**drank** 등

She **put** sugar in her coffee.
They **made** a big mistake.
I **came** back home after a trip.
The man **gave** some toys to me.

SPEED CHECK

( ) 안에서 알맞은 말을 고르시오.

1 I (weared / wore) a red dress yesterday.
2 Jason (teached / taught) English three years ago.
3 The baseball player (hitted / hit) the ball hard during the game.
4 Mindy (droped / dropped) the cup and (breaked / broke) it.

PRACTICE TEST

A 다음 밑줄 친 부분을 어법에 맞게 고치시오.

1 Jenny <u>hurries</u> to the bus stop last night.
2 We <u>have</u> a good time last Friday.
3 I <u>planed</u> a vacation yesterday.
4 Sam <u>losed</u> his smartphone last month.
5 Jake <u>calls</u> me two days ago.
6 She <u>readed</u> a novel last weekend.
7 They <u>live</u> here a few years ago.

A
hurry ⑧ 서둘러 가다
novel ⑲ 소설
a few 약간의, 몇몇의

B 다음 표의 내용과 일치하도록 문장을 완성하시오.

	last month	**last weekend**	**yesterday**
Ava	travel to Spain	chat online	go shopping
Ella	buy a tablet	eat Japanese food	watch a movie

1 Ava _____ _____ _____ last month.
2 Ella _____ _____ _____ last month.
3 Ava _____ _____ last weekend.
4 Ella _____ _____ _____ last weekend.
5 Yesterday, Ava _____ _____ and Ella _____ _____ _____.

B
travel ⑧ 여행하다
go shopping
쇼핑을 가다
tablet ⑲ 태블릿 PC,
휴대용 컴퓨터
Japanese ⑲ 일본의

C 우리말과 뜻이 같도록 보기의 말을 사용하여 문장을 완성하시오.

보기	hurt bring take hit

1 그는 아까 샤워를 했다.
   He _____ a shower a minute ago.

2 나는 그저께 내 어깨를 다쳤다.
   I _____ my shoulder the day before yesterday.

3 나는 어제 학교에 내 우산을 가져왔다.
   I _____ my umbrella to school yesterday.

4 한 시간 전에 강풍이 한국을 강타했다.
   Strong winds _____ Korea an hour ago.

C
shoulder ⑲ 어깨
the day before
yesterday 그저께
strong wind 강풍

일반동사가 있는 부정문

주어의 인칭과 수		부정	줄임말
현재	I/you/we/they 등 3인칭 단수 외	do not+동사원형	don't+동사원형
	he/she/it 등 3인칭 단수	does not+동사원형	doesn't+동사원형
과거	모든 인칭과 수	did not+동사원형	didn't+동사원형

1 『don't[do not]+동사원형』: 현재시제이며, 주어가 3인칭 단수가 아닌 모든 경우에 쓴다.

I **don't get up** early on weekends.

You **don't remember** my name.

Sam and Jenny **don't take** a bus to school.

2 『doesn't[does not]+동사원형』: 현재시제이며, 주어가 3인칭 단수일 때 쓴다.

He **doesn't eat** meat.

Logan **doesn't talk** much.

My dog **doesn't bark** all day.

3 『didn't[did not]+동사원형』: 주어의 인칭과 수에 관계없이 과거시제일 때 쓴다.

I **didn't play** smartphone games yesterday.

They **didn't feel** safe at that time.

She **didn't sleep** well last night.

Tip 비교! do not vs. don't

일반적으로 do not, does not, did not보다 줄임말 don't, doesn't, didn't를 더 자주 사용한다.

단, 부정의 의미를 강하게 표현할 때는 줄이지 않고 사용하기도 한다.

We **do not want** war. We want peace.

I **did not lie** to you.

SPEED CHECK

( ) 안에서 알맞은 말을 고르시오.

1 I (don't / doesn't) like loud music.

2 Mr. Davis (don't / doesn't) study art history.

3 They (don't / didn't) have a car last year.

4 We (don't / didn't) eat breakfast these days.

PRACTICE TEST

정답 및 해설 p.5

A 다음 Shopping List를 보고 빈칸에 알맞은 말을 쓰시오.

Susie's Shopping List	My Shopping List
bread, butter, apples, coffee	cheese, mango juice, rice, apples

1 Susie _____ have any butter. She needs some.

2 I _____ need coffee. I need some mango juice.

3 Susie _____ want rice. She wants some bread.

4 Susie and I _____ need oranges. We need apples.

B 주어진 동사의 부정형을 사용하여 문장을 완성하시오. (단, 줄임말을 쓸 것)

1 We _____ meat. We eat vegetables. (eat)

2 He _____ pizza. He likes steak. (like)

3 My mom _____ sugar. She uses honey. (use)

4 Glenn _____ tennis yesterday. He played soccer. (play)

5 I _____ a cooking class. I take a yoga class. (take)

6 The movie was not good. We _____ it. (enjoy)

7 My brother and I _____ at the party. We danced. (sing)

8 My washing machine _____. I'm worried. (work)

C 우리말과 뜻이 같도록 주어진 말을 사용하여 문장을 완성하시오.

1 나는 롤러코스터를 타지 않는다. (ride)

_____ _____ _____ roller coasters.

2 우리는 우리 방을 청소하지 않았다. (clean)

_____ _____ _____ our rooms.

3 그는 록 음악을 듣지 않는다. (listen to)

_____ _____ _____ _____ rock music.

4 그들은 저녁에 커피를 마시지 않는다. (drink, coffee)

_____ _____ _____ _____ in the evening.

5 그녀는 스페인어를 말하지 않는다. (speak, Spanish)

_____ _____ _____ _____ .

A
shopping list 쇼핑 목록
bread ⑲ 빵
butter ⑲ 버터
rice ⑲ 쌀

B
meat ⑲ 고기
vegetable ⑲ 채소
honey ⑲ 꿀
enjoy ⑧ 즐기다
washing machine
세탁기
worried ⑲ 걱정하는
work ⑧ 일하다; *작동하다

C
ride ⑧ 타다
clean ⑧ 청소하다
Spanish ⑲ 스페인어

일반동사가 있는 의문문

주어의 인칭과 수		의문문의 형태	대답	
			긍정	부정
현재	I/you/we/they 등 3인칭 단수 외	Do+주어+동사원형 ...?	Yes, 주어+do.	No, 주어+don't.
	he/she/it 등 3인칭 단수	Does+주어+동사원형 ...?	Yes, 주어+does.	No, 주어+doesn't.
과거	모든 인칭과 수	Did+주어+동사원형 ...?	Yes, 주어+did.	No, 주어+didn't.

A: **Do you run** every day?
B: **Yes, I do. / No, I don't.**

A: **Does the man read** the news every morning?
B: **Yes, he does. / No, he doesn't.**

A: **Did Riley arrive** on time?
B: **Yes, she did. / No, she didn't.**

1 『Do+주어+동사원형 ...?』: 현재시제이며, 주어가 3인칭 단수가 아닌 모든 경우에 쓴다.
   Do you want some milk? – **Yes, I do.**
   Do they like classical music? – **No, they don't.** They like pop music.

2 『Does+주어+동사원형 ...?』: 현재시제이며, 주어가 3인칭 단수일 때 쓴다.
   Does he wear glasses? – **Yes, he does.**
   Does she play the piano? – **No, she doesn't.** She plays the guitar.

3 『Did+주어+동사원형 ...?』: 주어의 인칭과 수에 관계없이 과거시제일 때 쓴다.
   Did you finish your homework? – **Yes, I did.**
   Did Lily go downtown last night? – **No, she didn't.** She stayed home.

SPEED CHECK

(   ) 안에서 알맞은 말을 고르시오.

1 (Do / Does) he live in London now?

2 (Do / Does) you wash your dog every day?

3 (Does / Did) Karen leave a message yesterday?

4 (Do / Does) we need sugar?

5 (Did / Do) they win the last game?

PRACTICE TEST

정답 및 해설 p.6

A 다음 밑줄 친 부분을 어법에 맞게 고치시오.

1 Does you study Chinese these days?

2 Do this bus stop at Central Park?

3 Did they enjoyed the jazz festival?

4 Does your sister gets up early?

B 다음 문장을 의문문으로 바꿔 쓰시오.

1 He made this pasta.

→ _____ he _____ this pasta?

2 Jennifer plays the drums.

→ _____ Jennifer _____ the drums?

3 She met her friends last Friday.

→ _____ she _____ her friends last Friday?

C 다음 대화가 성립하도록 질문에 대한 대답을 완성하시오.

1 A: Does he have a sister?

B: _____, _____ _____. He has a brother.

2 A: Do you often swim in the sea?

B: _____, _____ _____. I love swimming in the sea.

3 A: Did she go to the concert?

B: _____, _____ _____. She went to the movies.

D 우리말과 뜻이 같도록 주어진 말을 사용하여 대화를 완성하시오.

A: Robin은 그 박물관을 방문했니? (visit the museum)

A: _____ _____ _____ _____ _____?

B: 응, 그랬어.

B: _____, _____ _____.

A
Chinese ⑲ 중국어
festival ⑲ 축제
get up 일어나다

C
often ⑭ 자주
go to the movies
영화 보러 가다

D
visit ⑧ 방문하다
museum ⑲ 박물관

REVIEW TEST

01

| _____ hikes on weekends. |

① We   ② They
③ He   ④ I
⑤ Sally and Tony

02

| _____ they go on a picnic last weekend? |

① Does   ② Do
③ Were   ④ Was
⑤ Did

03

| He _____ Maya's birthday last year. |

① isn't forget   ② wasn't forget
③ doesn't forget   ④ didn't forget
⑤ don't forget

서술형

[04-05] 우리말과 뜻이 같도록 주어진 말을 바르게 배열하시오.

04 너는 어제 그 약을 먹었니?

(take, you, the medicine, did)

→ _____ yesterday?

05 나는 오늘 아침에 내 휴대 전화를 가져오지 않았다.

(I, cell phone, didn't, my, bring)

→ _____ this morning.

[06-07] B에 들어갈 대답으로 알맞은 것을 고르시오.

06

| A: Do you like cheesecake?
B: _____ I like chocolate cake. |

① No, I do.   ② No, I don't.
③ Yes, I do.   ④ Yes, I don't.
⑤ No, I'm not.

07

| A: Did he fight with his sister?
B: _____ |

① Yes, he was.   ② No, he wasn't.
③ No, he doesn't.   ④ No, he did.
⑤ Yes, he did.

08 다음 우리말을 영어로 바르게 옮긴 것은?

| 그녀는 슬픈 영화를 좋아하지 않는다. |

① She don't like sad movies.
② She didn't like sad movies.
③ She likes not sad movies.
④ She doesn't likes sad movies.
⑤ She doesn't like sad movies.

09 다음 빈칸에 들어갈 말을 바르게 짝지은 것은?

> A: ___ⓐ___ your father ___ⓑ___ in the hospital?
> B: Yes. He's a doctor.

	ⓐ	ⓑ		ⓐ	ⓑ
①	Do	– work	②	Does	– works
③	Does	– work	④	Do	– works
⑤	Did	– worked			

[10-11] 다음 밑줄 친 부분 중 어법상 **틀린** 것을 고르시오.

10 ① She usually <u>fixs</u> problems.
② Alice <u>rides</u> a bike every morning.
③ The boys <u>play</u> soccer after school.
④ Charlie <u>studies</u> Japanese very hard.
⑤ She <u>reads</u> a newspaper in the morning.

11 ① My students <u>don't</u> like math.
② <u>Did</u> you meet him last Thursday?
③ We <u>didn't</u> go shopping yesterday.
④ <u>Does</u> her parents know her friends?
⑤ <u>Did</u> he take many pictures in China?

서술형

[12-13] 다음 밑줄 친 부분을 어법에 맞게 고치시오.

12 He <u>buy</u> a pair of sneakers yesterday.

13 These days, Jennifer <u>went jogging</u> every morning.

서술형　NEW　내신 기출

14 다음 Henry의 일과표를 보고 글을 완성할 때 (A), (B), (C)에 들어갈 말을 조건에 맞게 쓰시오.

have lunch	at noon
come home from school	before 4:30
learn yoga	after dinner

─────| 조건 |─────
• 현재시제로 쓸 것
• 시간 순서에 맞게 쓸 것
• (A), (B), (C) 모두 각 4단어로 쓸 것

Henry (A) _____.
He (B) _____ before 4:30
every day. He (C) _____.

고난도　NEW　내신 기출

15 다음 중 어법상 옳은 것을 모두 고르면?

① We didn't say anything.
② My cousin doesn't eats sushi.
③ You don't have enough time.
④ He didn't worked here last year.
⑤ I use not an umbrella on rainy days.

[16-17] 다음 빈칸에 공통으로 들어갈 수 있는 말을 고르시오.

16

> A: Terry, _____ you do your homework last night?
> B: Yes, I _____. It was difficult.

① does　　　② do
③ did　　　④ was
⑤ are

19 다음 밑줄 친 부분 중 어법상 틀린 것은?

> Last Saturday we ① had a basketball game. We ② did our best, but we ③ losed. Our coach ④ cheered us up. We ⑤ decided to win the next game.

서술형

[20-22] 우리말과 뜻이 같도록 주어진 말을 사용하여 문장을 완성하시오.

20 나는 호주에서 캥거루들을 봤다. (see, kangaroos)

→ _____ _____ _____ in Australia.

17

> • Did she _____ the zoo?
> • We _____ our grandparents every month.

① visit　　　② visits
③ visited　　　④ not visit
⑤ doesn't visit

21 너는 네 조부모님으로부터 용돈을 받니?
(get, pocket money)

→ _____ _____ _____ _____
from your grandparents?

서술형

18 다음 Peter의 주말 일정을 보고 대화를 완성하시오.

Saturdays	Sundays
play chess with his dad	teach English to children

A: Does Peter play chess with his dad on Sundays?
B: _____, _____ _____. He _____
_____ _____ on Sundays.

22 Brian은 그의 형의 바지를 입었다. 그것들은 그에게 맞지 않았다. (wear, fit)
→ Brian _____ his brother's pants. They
_____ _____ him.

28

CHAPTER

03

명사와 관사

UNIT 1

셀 수 있는 명사와 셀 수 없는 명사

A 명사: mom, cup, school, peace 등과 같이 사람, 사물, 장소, 개념 등을 나타내는 말이다.

B 셀 수 있는 명사
- '하나, 둘, …'로 셀 수 있는 명사를 의미한다.
- 단수('하나') 명사 앞에는 부정관사 a/an을 쓴다.
- 복수('둘 이상') 명사는 대개 명사 뒤에 -s를 붙여 만들지만 불규칙하게 변하는 경우가 있다.

셀 수 있는 명사의 복수형 만드는 법		
대부분의 명사	명사+-s	books, maps, dogs, cats, bags 등
-s, -ss, -x, -ch, -sh, -o로 끝나는 명사	명사+-es	buses, kisses, boxes, watches, dishes, potatoes 등 〈예외〉 pianos, photos
'자음+-y'로 끝나는 명사	y를 i로 고치고+-es	lady → ladies, baby → babies, city → cities 등
'모음+-y'로 끝나는 명사	명사+-s	boys, toys, monkeys 등
-f, -fe로 끝나는 명사	f, fe를 v로 고치고+-es	leaf → leaves, knife → knives 등 〈예외〉 roofs
불규칙 변화		man-men, woman-women, foot-feet, tooth-teeth, child-children, mouse-mice, ox-oxen, goose-geese 등
단수와 복수가 같은 명사		sheep(a sheep, two sheep), fish, deer 등

C 셀 수 없는 명사
- '하나, 둘, …'로 셀 수 없는 명사를 의미한다.
- 셀 수 없는 명사 앞에는 부정관사 a/an을 쓰지 않는다.
- 단수형으로 쓰고 단수 취급한다.

1 셀 수 없는 명사의 종류
- 물질명사(나누어 셀 수 없는 물질): cheese, paper, water, milk, sugar, coffee, money, juice 등
- 추상명사(추상적인 개념): joy, happiness, luck, love, beauty, peace, time, music 등
- 고유명사(사람, 지역, 나라 이름 등): Emma, Washington, Korea 등

2 셀 수 없는 명사의 수량 표현: 단위나 용기, 모양 등을 나타내는 명사를 사용하여 수량을 나타낸다.
a piece of paper[cheese/furniture/cake/bread/pizza/advice], **a slice of** pizza[cheese/bread], **a cup of** coffee, **a bowl of** rice, **a loaf of** bread, **two bottles of** Coke, **six glasses of** water 등

1 glasses(안경), scissors(가위), pants(바지), shoes(신발) 등 똑같은 두 개의 부분이 하나를 이루는 명사는 항상 복수형으로 쓰며 단위를 나타내는 명사 pair로 수량을 표시한다. *e.g.* **a pair of** glasses, **two pairs of** glasses
2 물질명사의 경우 일상 대화에서는 원칙에 어긋나게 사용하기도 한다.
Two coffees, please.

SPEED CHECK

빈칸에 알맞은 말을 고르시오.

Danny drinks two _____ of milk every day.

① loaves   ② pieces   ③ pairs   ④ slices   ⑤ glasses

PRACTICE TEST

정답 및 해설 p.8

A ( ) 안에서 알맞은 말을 고르시오.

1 She smiled with (joy / a joy).

2 Busan and Jeju are (citys / cities) in Korea.

3 In the fall the (leafs / leaves) turn red and yellow.

4 I need (sugar / a sugar) for my coffee.

5 My (foots / feet) are very cold.

A
fall 몡 가을
turn 통 …로 변하다

B 다음 밑줄 친 부분을 어법에 맞게 고치시오.

1 <u>An air</u> is very important to us.

2 Ladies and <u>gentlemans</u>, attention, please!

3 The farmer has <u>three sheeps</u> on his farm.

B
important 혱 중요한
Attention, please.
주목해 주세요.
farmer 몡 농부
farm 몡 농장

C 보기의 말과 주어진 말을 사용하여 문장을 완성하시오. (단, 보기의 말은 한 번씩만 쓸 것)

| 보기 | slice   bowl   piece   glass   pair |

1 He had _____. (two, rice)

2 I used _____. (two, paper)

3 Jack drank _____. (five, water)

4 Sally ate _____. (three, pizza)

5 They bought _____. (a, pants)

D 우리말과 뜻이 같도록 주어진 말을 사용하여 문장을 완성하시오.

1 그 어부들이 물고기 두 마리를 잡았다. (fish)

   The fishermen caught _____ _____.

2 식탁 위에 토마토 세 개가 있다. (tomato)

   There are _____ _____ on the table.

3 그는 충고 한 마디를 요청했다. (advice)

   He asked for _____ _____ _____ _____.

4 운동장에 남자아이 다섯 명이 있다. (boy)

   There are _____ _____ on the playground.

D
fisherman 몡 어부
ask for …을 요청하다
playground 몡 운동장,
　　　　　　놀이터

UNIT 2 관사

A

관사: 명사 앞에서 명사의 의미와 성격을 드러내는 말로, 부정관사 a/an과 정관사 the가 있다.

B

관사의 종류와 생략

1 **부정관사 a/an**: 단수명사 앞에 쓴다. 뒤에 나오는 명사의 발음이 자음으로 시작하면 a, 모음으로 시작하면 an을 쓴다.

e.g. **a** student, **a** university, **a** week, **an** orange, **an** hour 등

1) **막연한 하나를 나타낼 때**: He is **a** tourist.

2) **'하나의(one)'**: I have **a** son.

3) **'…마다/에/당'(= per)**: The car goes 60 km **an** hour.

2 **정관사 the**

1) 앞서 나온 명사를 가리킬 때

He bought a new car. **The** car was great.

2) 서로 아는 것을 가리키거나 정황상 무엇인지 알 수 있을 때

Open **the** door, please.

3) 명사가 수식어의 꾸밈을 받아 특정한 것을 가리킬 때

The letter *on the desk* is yours.

4) 기타: play **the** piano (악기명), **the** sun/sky/earth/world (하나뿐인 존재), **the** sea/rain/weather (환경, 기후 등), **the** Internet (인터넷) 등

I play **the** violin well. (바이올린이라는 악기를 연주한다는 의미)

> **Tip 비교!** I have **a** violin. (막연한 바이올린 하나를 의미)

3 **관사의 생략**

1) **식사명 앞에서**: after lunch, have dinner 등

> **Tip 비교!** 식사명 breakfast, lunch, dinner 등에는 관사를 쓰지 않는 것이 보통이나, 앞에 수식하는 말이 올 때는 부정관사 a/an을 쓰기도 한다.
> Have **a** *nice* dinner.

2) **운동 경기명 앞에서**: play tennis/soccer/baseball/basketball 등

3) **『by+교통/통신 수단』에서**: by bus/taxi/train/email 등

4) **건물이나 장소가 본래의 용도로 쓰일 때**: go to school/bed/church(등교하다/잠자리에 들다/교회에 가다) 등

SPEED CHECK

빈칸에 알맞은 말을 고르시오.

1 The dolphin is _____ clever animal.

① a ② an ③ the ④ by ⑤ 필요 없음

2 He plays _____ soccer very well.

① a ② an ③ the ④ by ⑤ 필요 없음

PRACTICE TEST

정답 및 해설 p.8

A a, an, the 중 알맞은 말을 빈칸에 쓰시오.

1 Could you hold _____ door?
2 _____ weather is very good today.
3 Jenny is _____ orchestra member.
4 Kate plays _____ flute after school.
5 Brian saw _____ elephant at a circus.
6 _____ moon goes around _____ earth.
7 She visits her grandparents' house once _____ month.

A
hold ⑧ 잡다
weather ⑲ 날씨
orchestra ⑲ 오케스트라,
　　　　　　관현악단
circus ⑲ 서커스
go around
…의 주위를 돌다
once ⑨ 한 번

B 다음 밑줄 친 부분을 어법에 맞게 고치시오.

1 I have a idea for our project.
2 They work eight hours the day.
3 My parents went to the hospital by a taxi.
4 I chatted with my friend on an Internet.
5 We had good dinner last night.
6 I like a bakery on the corner.
7 I bought a winter coat. A coat is very warm.

B
project ⑲ 프로젝트, 계획
bakery ⑲ 빵집, 제과점
corner ⑲ 모퉁이

C 우리말과 뜻이 같도록 주어진 말을 사용하여 문장을 완성하시오.

1 우리는 태양 아래에서 휴식을 취했다. (sun)
　 We took a break in _____ _____.

2 냄비 안에 있는 물은 매우 뜨겁다. (water)
　 _____ _____ in the pot is very hot.

3 Sam은 매주 토요일 오전에 테니스를 친다. (play, tennis)
　 Sam _____ _____ every Saturday morning.

4 그녀는 일주일에 6일을 스케이팅 연습을 한다. (week)
　 She practices skating six days _____ _____.

5 나는 버스를 타고 학교에 간다. (school, bus)
　 I _____ _____ _____ _____ _____.

C
take a break
휴식을 취하다
pot ⑲ 냄비
practice ⑧ 연습하다

REVIEW TEST

01 다음 중 성격이 나머지와 <u>다른</u> 것은?

① love　　　② air

③ milk　　　④ map

⑤ joy

02 다음 중 명사의 복수형이 바르게 연결된 것은?

① fish – fishes　　② baby – babys

③ child – childs　　④ tooth – teeths

⑤ woman – women

03 다음 빈칸에 들어갈 수 <u>없는</u> 것은?

I need a piece of _____ .

① paper　　　② cheese

③ cake　　　④ advice

⑤ water

서술형

[04-05] 다음 문장에서 <u>틀린</u> 부분을 찾아 바르게 고치시오.

04 A flower in the vase is a rose.

(　　　　　) → (　　　　　)

05 I put my books on some shelfs.

(　　　　　) → (　　　　　)

[06-07] 다음 빈칸에 들어갈 말을 바르게 짝지은 것을 고르시오.

06

Ms. Smith has ___ⓐ___ sports car. ___ⓑ___ car is really nice.

　　　ⓐ　　ⓑ　　　　　ⓐ　　ⓑ

① an – The　　② a – The

③ a – A　　　④ the – A

⑤ the – The

07

ⓐ _____ sun rises in the east.
ⓑ It was _____ interesting game.
ⓒ I play _____ guitar in a band.

　　　ⓐ　　ⓑ　　ⓒ

① The – an – a

② The – an – the

③ The – a – a

④ An – the – a

⑤ An – a – the

08 다음 밑줄 친 부분 중 어법상 <u>틀린</u> 것은?

Liz and <u>her friend</u> <u>had pizza</u> and two <u>bowls</u>
　　　　　①　　　　②　　　　　　③
of <u>salads</u> <u>for lunch</u>.
　　④　　⑤

09 다음 중 빈칸에 a나 an을 쓸 수 <u>없는</u> 것은?

① She is _____ Ann.

② The baby has _____ cute smile.

③ He is _____ English teacher.

④ Alex studied hard for _____ exam.

⑤ I bought _____ apple pie yesterday.

10 다음 중 빈칸에 An[an]이 들어갈 수 <u>없는</u> 문장의 개수는?

ⓐ Is she _____ artist?
ⓑ Don't go out in _____ rain.
ⓒ _____ hour has sixty minutes.
ⓓ _____ elephant has a long nose.
ⓔ Kevin took medicine twice _____ day.

① 1개   ② 2개   ③ 3개
④ 4개   ⑤ 5개

11 다음 우리말을 영어로 바르게 옮긴 것은?

벽에 있는 그 거울은 내 것이다.

① Mirror on the wall is mine.
② A mirror on the wall is mine.
③ An mirror on the wall is mine.
④ The mirror on the wall is mine.
⑤ The mirror is mine on the wall.

[12-13] 다음 밑줄 친 부분 중 어법상 <u>틀린</u> 것을 고르시오.

12 ① The boy plays with <u>toys</u>.
② The farmer grows <u>tomatoes</u>.
③ I saw two <u>deers</u> in the forest.
④ I traveled to many <u>cities</u> in the USA.
⑤ There are 11 <u>players</u> on a soccer team.

13 ① His name is <u>Bob</u>.
② We pray for <u>peace</u>.
③ Stella is from <u>Canada</u>.
④ I wish him <u>good luck</u>.
⑤ Jacob found <u>happinesses</u> in his life.

14 다음 중 빈칸에 the를 쓸 수 <u>없는</u> 것은?

① Turn on _____ TV, please.
② I went there by _____ taxi.
③ Jasmin played _____ cello.
④ I want to travel around _____ world.
⑤ Will you close _____ door behind you?

15 다음 쇼핑 목록을 보고 주어진 말을 사용하여 문장을 완성하시오.

My Shopping List

1) I need _____ _____. (dish)
2) I need _____ _____ _____ _____, too. (shoes)
3) Also, I want _____ _____ _____ _____ from the bakery. (bread)

16 다음 대화의 빈칸에 들어갈 수 있는 것은?

A: What would you like to order?
B: I'd like a steak.
A: Anything to drink?
B: _____, please.

① Glass of wine   ② Glass of wines
③ Glasses of wines   ④ A glass of wine
⑤ The glass of wine

17 다음 중 어법상 옳은 것을 바르게 짝지은 것은?

> ⓐ Please pass me a salt.
> ⓑ Monkeys live in groups.
> ⓒ Many people surf an Internet.
> ⓓ The meetings are once a month.
> ⓔ The blouse in the drawer is Jessica's.

① ⓐ, ⓑ   ② ⓑ, ⓓ   ③ ⓑ, ⓒ, ⓓ

④ ⓑ, ⓓ, ⓔ   ⑤ ⓐ, ⓓ, ⓔ

[18-20] 우리말과 뜻이 같도록 주어진 말을 사용하여 문장을 완성하시오.

18 나는 지난 주말에 안경을 하나 샀다. (glasses)

→ I bought _____ _____ _____ _____

last weekend.

19 고양이가 정원에서 두 마리의 쥐를 뒤쫓았다. (mouse)

→ The cat chased _____ _____ in the garden.

20 나는 지구에 관한 책을 한 권 샀다. 그 책은 두껍다.

(book, earth)

→ I bought _____ _____ about _____

_____. _____ is thick.

21 다음 중 어법상 옳은 것은 모두 몇 개인가?

> ⓐ A love is important.
> ⓑ We went to the sea last summer.
> ⓒ Veronica has many watches.
> ⓓ He goes jogging before the breakfast.

① 1개   ② 2개   ③ 3개

④ 4개   ⑤ 없음

22 다음 우리말을 영어로 옮길 때 세 번째 오는 말은?

> 나는 내 친구들과 농구를 했다.

① played   ② the

③ basketball   ④ with

⑤ friends

23 다음 조건에 맞게 문장을 써넣어 대화를 완성하시오.

> A: Do you know Charlie Puth?
> B: Sure. _____
>   (그는 유명한 가수야.)

> ┤ 조건 ├
> • 우리말 뜻에 맞게 문장을 완성할 것
> • 알맞은 관사와 famous를 사용하여 쓸 것
> • 5단어의 완전한 문장으로 쓸 것

24 우리말과 뜻이 같도록 주어진 말을 사용하여 대화를 완성하시오.

A: 나의 삼촌은 매주 30시간 수영을 해. (hour, week)

B: Wow! He is really amazing!

→ My uncle swims 30 _____ _____.

CHAPTER

04

문장의 시제

UNIT 1 현재시제와 과거시제

현재시제: 현재의 상태나 사실, 일상적인 습관이나 반복되는 일, 변하지 않는 사실이나 과학적 사실, 격언 등을 나타낸다.

1 현재의 상태나 사실

There **is** a lemon tree in the garden. (현재의 상태)

She **studies** law in university. (현재의 사실)

2 일상적인 습관이나 반복되는 일

Ann **spends** time with her family on weekends.

3 변하지 않는 사실이나 과학적 사실

Two plus five **is** seven.

Water **boils** at 100 °C.

과거시제: 과거의 동작이나 상태, 역사적 사실 등을 나타낸다.

1 과거에 이미 끝난 동작이나 상태

I **gave** her a book for her birthday. (과거의 동작)

My favorite actor **was** on TV yesterday. (과거의 상태)

2 역사적 사실

World War I **ended** in 1918.

> 과거시제는 흔히 과거를 나타내는 시간의 부사(구)와 함께 쓴다.
> yesterday, last night[week, month, year, Monday 등], ago 등
> Kate **went** to the museum *last Saturday*.

Grammar UP **미래시제:** 미래에 발생할 일을 나타낼 때는 『will+동사원형』이나 『be going to+동사원형』을 쓴다. (CHAPTER 05 참고)

I **will be** 15 years old next year.

They **are going to get** married next month.

 SPEED CHECK

빈칸에 알맞은 말을 고르시오.

1 My father _____ the news online every day.

　① reading　　　② reads　　　③ be reading　　　④ is reads　　　⑤ has read

2 They _____ to Hawaii two years ago.

　① move　　　② moves　　　③ moved　　　④ moving　　　⑤ are moving

3 Mother Teresa _____ in 1997.

　① die　　　② dies　　　③ died　　　④ is dying　　　⑤ has died

PRACTICE TEST

A ( ) 안에서 알맞은 말을 고르시오.

1 Plants (needed / need) water and light.
2 The couple (have / had) a good dinner last night.
3 Mr. Brown (read / reads) the book a year ago.
4 What's wrong? You (look / looked) sad now.
5 Allie (buys / bought) a cell phone last year.

A
plant ⑲ 식물
light ⑲ 빛
wrong ⑲ 잘못된

B 다음 밑줄 친 부분을 어법에 맞게 고치시오.

1 Last summer <u>is</u> very hot.
2 Three plus seven <u>was</u> ten.
3 The Wright brothers <u>invents</u> the airplane in 1903.
4 <u>Do they play</u> soccer last Sunday?
5 I get up early and <u>ate</u> breakfast every morning.

B
invent ⑧ 발명하다

C 우리말과 뜻이 같도록 주어진 말을 사용하여 문장을 완성하시오.

1 Ottawa는 캐나다의 수도이다. (the capital)
Ottawa _____ _____ _____ of Canada.

2 Mary는 매일 아침 샤워를 한다. (take a shower)
_____ _____ _____ _____ every morning.

3 그 기차는 10분 전에 떠났다. (the train, leave)
_____ _____ _____ 10 minutes ago.

4 나는 어젯밤에 내 사진을 게시했다. (post, my picture)
_____ _____ _____ _____ last night.

5 나는 새 드레스를 샀다. 나는 행복했다. (buy a new dress, be)
I _____ _____ _____ _____. I _____ happy.

6 Mozart는 많은 곡들을 썼다. Mia는 매일 그것들을 듣는다.
(write many songs, listen to)
Mozart _____ _____ _____. Mia _____ _____ them every day.

C
capital ⑲ 수도
take a shower
샤워를 하다
leave ⑧ 떠나다
(leave-left)

진행형

A

진행형: 특정 시점에서 진행 중인 일을 나타낸다.

1 현재 진행형('…하고 있다'): 『be동사의 현재형(am/are/is)+v-ing』

Sam **is playing** baseball with his friends.

The guests **are dancing** at the party.

2 과거 진행형('…하고 있었다'): 『be동사의 과거형(was/were)+v-ing』

Frank **was writing** an email.

My friends **were reading** comic books.

3 v-ing를 만드는 법

대부분의 동사	동사원형+-ing	do-do**ing**, go-go**ing**, eat-eat**ing**, play-play**ing**, talk-talk**ing**, read-read**ing**, walk-walk**ing**, learn-learn**ing** 등
-e로 끝나는 동사	e를 빼고+-ing	come-com**ing**, live-liv**ing**, make-mak**ing**, skate-skat**ing**, write-writ**ing**, take-tak**ing**, smile-smil**ing** 등
-ie로 끝나는 동사	ie를 y로 고치고+-ing	die-d**ying**, lie-l**ying**, tie-t**ying** 등
'단모음+단자음'으로 끝나고 그 단모음에 강세가 있는 동사	자음을 한 번 더 쓰고 +-ing	cut-cut**ting**, sit-sit**ting**, get-get**ting**, begin-begin**ning**, stop-stop**ping**, run-run**ning**, swim-swim**ming** 등

B

진행형의 부정문과 의문문

1 부정문: 『be동사+not v-ing』

I'**m not listening** to music. I'm listening to the news.

We **were not taking** a picture.

2 의문문: 『be동사+주어+v-ing …?』

Are you studying for the math test? – **Yes, I am.**

Was he watching TV at that time? – **No, he wasn't.**

> **Tip 주의!** 소유나 상태를 나타내는 동사는 진행형으로 쓰지 않는다. *e.g.* have, know, want 등
> I **know** him. (← I'**m knowing** him.)
> I **have** a car. (← I'**m having** a car.)
> • 단, have가 '먹다'의 뜻으로 쓰일 경우 진행형으로 쓸 수 있다. I'**m having** pizza now.

SPEED CHECK

빈칸에 알맞은 말을 고르시오.

1 Nancy _____ a sandwich now.

① make   ② made   ③ making   ④ are making   ⑤ is making

2 _____ you _____ the magazine?

① Are, reading   ② Be, reading   ③ Are, read   ④ Is, reading   ⑤ Do, reading

PRACTICE TEST

정답 및 해설 p.11

A 다음 Julia와 Dan이 어제 한 일을 보고 문장을 완성하시오.

	7:00 – 7:20 a.m.	8:00 – 8:15 a.m.	12:00 – 1:00 p.m.
Julia	wash her face	put on her uniform	have lunch
Dan	have breakfast	pack his school bag	have lunch

1 Julia _____ _____ _____ at 7:05 a.m.
2 Dan _____ _____ _____ at 7:10 a.m.
3 Julia _____ _____ _____ _____ at 8:10 a.m.
4 Dan _____ _____ _____ _____ at 8:10 a.m.
5 Julia and Dan _____ _____ _____ at 12:30 p.m.

A
wash one's face
세수하다
put on …을 입다
uniform 몡 유니폼, 교복
pack 통 (짐을) 싸다

B 우리말과 뜻이 같도록 주어진 말을 바르게 배열하시오.

1 너는 네 개를 산책시키고 있었니? (walking, you, were)
_____ your dog?

2 그들은 박수를 치고 있었다. (clapping, they, were)
_____ their hands.

3 그녀는 저녁을 준비하고 있지 않다. (preparing, not, she, is)
_____ dinner.

4 그가 나를 보고 미소 짓고 있었니? (smiling, he, was)
_____ at me?

B
walk 통 걷다; *(동물을)
산책시키다
clap one's hands
박수 치다
prepare 통 준비하다

C 우리말과 뜻이 같도록 주어진 말을 사용하여 문장을 완성하시오. (단, 부정문은 줄임말을 쓸 것)

1 너는 문 뒤에 숨어 있었니? (hide)
_____ _____ _____ behind the door?

2 나의 여동생은 프랑스어를 배우고 있다. (learn)
_____ _____ _____ _____ French.

3 그들은 소파에 앉아 있지 않았다. 그들은 뛰고 있었다. (sit, run)
_____ _____ _____ on the sofa. _____ _____ _____ .

C
hide 통 숨다
learn 통 배우다

REVIEW TEST

[01-03] 다음 빈칸에 들어갈 수 있는 말을 고르시오.

01

> The meeting _____ five minutes ago.

① begin　　　　　② began
③ begins　　　　④ is beginning
⑤ will begin

02

> They were _____ hamburgers in a fast-food restaurant.

① eat　　　　　② eats
③ eating　　　　④ ate
⑤ has eaten

03

> It _____ dark and cold now.

① got　　　　　② is getting
③ are getting　④ was getting
⑤ were getting

서술형

04 다음 대화의 빈칸에 알맞은 말을 쓰시오.

A: Did you find anything under the sofa?
B: Yes, I _____ a hairpin.

서술형

[05-06] 다음 문장에서 <u>틀린</u> 부분을 찾아 바르게 고치시오.

05 I am having an old camera.
　(　　　　　) → (　　　　　)

06 I was wanting a new pair of pants.
　(　　　　　) → (　　　　　)

NEW　**내신 기출**

07 다음 빈칸에 들어갈 수 있는 것을 모두 고르면?

> We cleaned the garden _____.

① now　　　　　② tomorrow
③ last month　　④ an hour ago
⑤ next weekend

서술형

08 주어진 말을 어법에 맞게 바꿔 쓰시오.

A: I'm tired. I _____ my uncle last night. (visit)
B: I'm tired too. I _____ tennis with my father yesterday. (practice)

09 B에 들어갈 대답으로 알맞은 것은?

> A: Are you watching a sci-fi movie?
> B: _____ I'm watching a horror movie.

① Yes, I do.　　　　② Yes, I am.
③ No, I don't.　　　④ No, I'm not.
⑤ Yes, I'm not.

12

A: _____ Jason _____ _____ _____?
　　(tie, his shoe)
B: Yes, he is.

10 다음 빈칸에 들어갈 말을 바르게 짝지은 것은?

> A: ____ⓐ____ you see him yesterday afternoon?
> B: No. I ____ⓑ____ him this morning.

|　　ⓐ　　　　ⓑ　　　　　　ⓐ　　　ⓑ|
① Did　–　see　　　② Do　–　see
③ Did　–　saw　　　④ Do　–　saw
⑤ Were　–　was

13

A: Was Emily reading a book?
B: _____, _____ _____. She _____ _____ a picture. (draw)

[11-13] 다음 그림을 보고 진행형과 주어진 말을 사용하여 대화를 완성하시오.

11

A: Is Susie in the kitchen?
B: Yes, she is. She _____ _____ _____ _____. (make, a cake)

14 다음 표를 보고 문장을 완성하시오.

	yesterday	**every day**
Ian	have a birthday party	clean his room
Sam	play basketball	go to the gym
Mia	finish the report	feed her dog

1) Every day Ian _____ _____ _____.
2) Sam _____ _____ yesterday.
3) Sam _____ _____ _____ _____ every day.
4) Mia _____ _____ _____ every day.

15
① I am eating not steak.

② The baby wasn't crying.

③ The sun rises in the east.

④ Is Tom cooking in the kitchen?

⑤ She had a great time last night.

16
① I am going to exercise at 7.

② My brother is really upset.

③ Are you sleeping at that time?

④ The Korean War ended in 1953.

⑤ My family is having dinner together.

서술형 **NEW** 내신 기출

17 우리말과 뜻이 같도록 주어진 철자로 시작하여 문장을 완성하시오.

그들은 바다에서 수영하고 있었다.

→ T_____ w_____ s_____ i_____ t_____
s_____.

[18-19] 다음 우리말을 영어로 바르게 옮긴 것을 고르시오.

18

| 우리 가족은 기차로 여행 중이다. |

① My family travel by train.

② My family travels by train.

③ My family traveled by train.

④ My family is traveling by train.

⑤ My family will travel by train.

19

| 그들은 노래하고 있지 않았다. |

① They don't sing.

② They didn't sing.

③ They aren't singing.

④ They weren't singing.

⑤ They are not going to sing.

고난도

20 다음 중 어법상 옳은 것은?

① Four plus four were eight.

② She was not skiing at that time.

③ They are going to the park yesterday.

④ Paul is taking not an after-class lesson.

⑤ King Sejong the Great invents Hangeul.

서술형 고난도

21 다음 글을 읽고, 어법상 **틀린** 문장을 모두 골라 바르게 고치시오.

It is Friday afternoon now. ① Mr. Brown is teaching English to his students. ② But they are not study hard. ③ They want a break. ④ Mr. Brown is knowing it. ⑤ 없음

CHAPTER

05

조동사

UNIT 1 will

조동사

• 동사 앞에 쓰여 미래, 가능, 허락, 추측, 의무 등의 뜻을 더하는 말이다.

• 주어의 인칭과 수에 관계없이 형태가 변하지 않는다.

• 두 개의 조동사를 연달아 쓸 수 없다.

• 평서문 『조동사＋동사원형』, 부정문 『조동사＋not＋동사원형』, 의문문 『조동사＋주어＋동사원형 …?』

1 will: '…할 것이다' (미래시제), '…하겠다' (의지)

It **will** *rain* tomorrow. (미래시제)

He**'ll**[He **will**] *be* busy tomorrow.

I **will** *change* his mind. (의지)

Karen **won't**[**will not**] *break* her promise.

Will you *go* skating? – **Yes, I will. / No, I won't.**

> **Tip 비교!** 『be going to + 동사원형』: '…할 것이다' (가까운 미래, 계획)
>
> We **are going to** *miss* you. (가까운 미래)
>
> She **is going to** *visit* us this weekend. (가까운 미래·계획)
>
> He**'s not going to** *stay up* all night.
>
> **Are** you **going to** *call* her? – **Yes, I am. / No, I'm not.**

> **Grammar UP** will의 과거형 would
>
> **1 과거 시점에서 미래를 나타낼 때**
>
>   He *said* that he **would** *meet* her.
>
> **2 정중한 부탁을 나타낼 때:** 『Would you＋동사원형 …?』
>
>   **Would you carry** my bags to the room?
>
> **3 『would like to＋동사원형』: '…하고 싶다'**
>
>   I**'d like to travel** around the world. (축약형: -'d like to)

SPEED CHECK

빈칸에 알맞은 말을 고르시오.

1 Jacob will _____ the kitchen next weekend.

① paint   ② paints   ③ painting   ④ painted   ⑤ is painting

2 Her speech is going to _____ in five minutes.

① ends   ② end   ③ ending   ④ ended   ⑤ is ending

3 I _____ going to have dinner.

① not   ② be not   ③ am not   ④ will   ⑤ won't

PRACTICE TEST

정답 및 해설 p.12

A ( ) 안에서 알맞은 말을 고르시오.

1 The sky will (is / be) clear this afternoon.
2 Is Angela going (clean / to clean) her room tonight?
3 Jim and Pam (is going to / are going to) take tennis lessons.
4 Kevin will (not study / study not) math today.
5 Will Michael (washes / wash) his dog this afternoon?
6 Oscar (is not going to / is going to not) take a bus.

A
clear ⑧ (날씨가) 맑은

B 다음 문장을 ( ) 안의 지시대로 바꿔 쓰시오.

1 Brian washes the dishes for his mom. (will을 사용한 미래시제)

→ _____

2 The train leaves on time. (will을 사용한 부정문)

→ _____

3 She helps me this weekend. (be going to를 사용한 의문문)

→ _____

4 We buy concert tickets. (be going to를 사용한 미래시제)

→ _____

5 Jenny cooks dinner. (be going to를 사용한 부정문)

→ _____

B
wash the dishes
설거지를 하다
on time 시간을 어기지 않고,
정각에

C 우리말과 뜻이 같도록 주어진 말을 사용하여 문장을 완성하시오.

1 너는 오늘 밤에 나한테 전화할 거니? (will, call me)
_____ _____ _____ _____ tonight?

2 너는 아이스크림을 먹을 거니? (be going to, eat)
_____ _____ _____ _____ _____ ice cream?

3 내 친구들은 그 파티에 오지 않을 것이다. (will, come)
_____ _____ _____ _____ to the party.

4 Julie는 오늘 저녁에 빨래하지 않을 것이다. (be going to, do laundry)
Julie _____ _____ _____ _____ _____ _____ this evening.

5 에어컨을 좀 꺼 주시겠어요? (would, turn off)
_____ _____ _____ _____ the air conditioner?

C
do laundry 빨래하다
turn off …을 끄다
air conditioner 에어컨

can, may

1 can

1) **능력·가능을 나타내는 can:** '…할 수 있다' (= be able to)

She **can** *speak* three languages.
   (= is able to)

Can you *swim*? – **Yes, I can. / No, I can't.**

I **cannot[can't]** *open* the file.
   (= am not able to)

2) **허가를 나타내는 can:** '…해도 좋다' (= may)

Can I *use* your cell phone? – **Yes, you can. / No, you can't.**

You **can't** *go* there alone.

> **Tip 주의!** 조동사 can은 미래를 나타낼 때 『will be able to+동사원형』을 쓴다.
>
> You **will be able to** *understand* it someday.
>
> (← ~~You will can understand it someday.~~)

> ✓**Grammar**
> **UP**
>
> can의 과거형 could
>
> **1** 과거 시점에서 능력을 나타낼 때
>
>   I *thought* Jason **could** speak English.
>
> **2** 공손한 부탁을 나타낼 때: 『Could you+동사원형 …?』
>
>   **Could you** *pass* me the salt?

2 may

1) **허가를 나타내는 may:** '…해도 좋다' (can보다 좀 더 정중한 표현)

You **may** *borrow* the dictionary.

You **may not** *copy* others' ideas.

May I *go* to the bathroom? – **Yes, you may. / No, you may not.**

2) **추측을 나타내는 may:** '…일지도 모른다'

The guests **may** *arrive* soon.

The rumor **may not** *be* true.

SPEED CHECK

빈칸에 알맞은 말을 고르시오.

1 _____ I sit here? – Yes, you may.

① Do   ② Am   ③ May   ④ Will   ⑤ Am able to

2 This washing machine _____ dry clothes.

① is   ② has   ③ do   ④ can   ⑤ is able

PRACTICE TEST

A 다음 밑줄 친 부분을 어법에 맞게 고치시오.

1 Kevin may be not late.
2 May I takes your order?
3 Are you able drive a car?
4 Eric may has enough money.
5 Can you to lend this book to me?
6 She was able not to solve the puzzle.

A
order (명) 주문
enough (형) 충분한
lend (동) 빌려주다
solve (동) 풀다, 해결하다
puzzle (명) 퍼즐, 수수께끼

B 보기의 말과 주어진 조동사를 사용하여 문장을 완성하시오.

| 보기 | go walk try read pass take |

1 I'm bored. _____ I _____ to the movies? (can)
2 You are in a museum. You _____ _____ _____ pictures here. (may)
3 Linda broke her leg. She _____ _____ for a month. (can't)
4 I didn't study hard. I _____ _____ _____ the exam. (may)
5 I like this sweater. _____ I _____ it on? (may)
6 This letter is for Sue. You _____ _____ it. (can't)

B
pass (동) 통과하다, 합격하다
bored (형) 지루해하는
museum (명) 박물관
break one's leg
다리가 부러지다
letter (명) 편지

C 우리말과 뜻이 같도록 주어진 말을 사용하여 문장을 완성하시오.

1 제가 물 한 잔을 마셔도 되나요? (have)
_____ _____ _____ a glass of water?

2 그는 탱고를 출 수 있다. (dance)
_____ _____ _____ the tango.

3 그는 매운 음식을 먹을 수 있니? (eat)
_____ _____ _____ _____ _____ spicy food?

4 내 친구는 그 선물을 좋아하지 않을지도 모른다. (like)
_____ _____ _____ _____ _____ the gift.

C
dance the tango
탱고를 추다
spicy (형) 매운
gift (명) 선물

must, should

1 must

1) 의무를 나타내는 must: '…해야 한다' (= have to)

You **must** *drive* slowly.
　　(= have to)
You **must not** *tell* lies.

> 의무를 나타내는 have to: '…해야 한다' (= must)
> She **has to** *go* home before dark.
> **Do** we **have to** *leave* now? – **Yes, we do. / No, we don't.**
>
> > Tip 주의! have to의 부정: don't[doesn't] have to ('…할 필요가 없다')
> > You **don't have to** *wait* for me.

2) 강한 추측을 나타내는 must: '…임이 틀림없다'

The old woman **must** *be* rich.
↔ The old woman **cannot[can't]** *be* rich. (cannot[can't]: '…일 리가 없다')

2 should: '…해야 한다' (must보다 강제성이 약한 의무, 충고, 제안)

We **should** *keep* our promises. (의무)
You **shouldn't[should not]** *trust* him. (충고)
You **should** *come* to the party. (제안)

> ✓ Grammar UP 「had better+동사원형」: '…하는 것이 낫다' (강한 충고나 권고)
> You'**d better take** some medicine. You're coughing a lot. (축약형: -'d better)
>
> > Tip 주의! had better는 형태는 과거이나 뜻은 현재이다.

SPEED CHECK

빈칸에 알맞은 말을 고르시오.

1 We _____ to work late tonight.

　① can　　　　　② will　　　　　③ must　　　　　④ have　　　　　⑤ should

2 Kathy didn't eat breakfast. She _____ be hungry.

　① cannot　　　② must　　　　　③ should　　　　④ had better　　⑤ have to

3 You _____ not watch too much TV.

　① have　　　　② won't　　　　③ should　　　　④ have to　　　　⑤ are able to

PRACTICE TEST

정답 및 해설 p.13

A (   ) 안에서 알맞은 말을 고르시오.

1 Robin (doesn't have / has not) to come early.

2 You should (not be / be not) rude to others.

3 Students (have to / have not to) follow the school rules.

4 He got a bad grade. He (must / cannot) be upset now.

5 I feel good. I (must not / don't have to) go to the hospital.

A
rude (형) 무례한
follow (동) 따르다
rule (명) 규칙
grade (명) 등급; *점수
hospital (명) 병원

B 다음 대화의 빈칸에 알맞은 말을 쓰시오.

1 A: Do I have to pack a coat?
　　B: Sure! It _____ be very cold in Sweden.

2 A: Should I call him back now?
　　B: Yes, you _____.

3 A: Do I have to go to the supermarket now?
　　B: No, you _____ _____ _____. We still have some milk.

4 A: I have a headache.
　　B: That's too bad. You'd _____ get some rest.

5 A: I broke my sister's phone. Should I tell her?
　　B: Of course. You _____ tell her the truth.

B
headache (명) 두통
get some rest
약간의 휴식을 취하다
truth (명) 진실, 사실

C 우리말과 뜻이 같도록 보기의 말과 주어진 말을 사용하여 문장을 완성하시오.

보기	must not didn't have to cannot has to

1 너는 여기에 주차하면 안 된다. (park)
_____ _____ _____ _____ here.

2 Molly는 신선한 과일을 더 많이 먹어야 한다. (eat)
_____ _____ _____ _____ more fresh fruit.

3 그는 모델일 리가 없다. (be)
_____ _____ _____ a model.

4 그들은 서두를 필요가 없었다. (hurry)
_____ _____ _____ _____ _____.

C
park (동) 주차하다
fresh (형) 신선한
model (명) 모형; *모델
hurry (동) 서두르다

REVIEW TEST

[01-02] 다음 밑줄 친 부분과 바꿔 쓸 수 있는 말을 고르시오.

01

> My parrot <u>is able to</u> talk.

① must ② should
③ had better ④ can
⑤ will

02

> You <u>can</u> call me Bill.

① must ② may
③ had better ④ are going to
⑤ will

[03-04] 다음 빈칸에 들어갈 수 있는 말을 고르시오.

03

> A: Can you go to the market with me?
> B: I'm sorry, _____.

① I will ② I can
③ I am not ④ I can't
⑤ I don't

04

> He _____ to an amusement park tomorrow.

① went ② did go
③ going ④ goes
⑤ will go

NEW 내신 기출

05 다음 우리말을 영어로 옮겨 쓸 때 사용되지 <u>않는</u> 표현은?

> Sally는 오늘 밤 파티에 올 것이다.

① to ② will
③ comes ④ tonight
⑤ the party

서술형

06 다음 표를 보고 대화를 완성하시오.

	the violin	**the ukulele**
James	×	×
Brian	○	×

James: Brian, can you play the violin?
Brian: _____, _____ _____. But _____
_____ play the ukulele. Can you play
the ukulele?
James: _____, _____ _____. _____ _____
play the violin either.

서술형

07 보기의 조동사를 한 번씩만 사용하여 문장을 완성하시오.

> ─── | 보기 | ───
> may   can   must   will   should

1) Dinner _____ be ready soon.
2) You _____ not eat so much fast food.
3) You had a long day. You _____ be tired.
4) We _____ read German but we can't
   speak it yet.
5) Excuse me, _____ I have a glass of water?
   I'm thirsty.

[08-09] 다음 중 어법상 틀린 것을 고르시오.

08 ① You had better take a bus.

② Theresa can't swim across the river.

③ She doesn't have to go to the store.

④ Children must not run indoors.

⑤ They're going not to have a meeting today.

09 ① Would you turn the volume down?

② I'd like to going fishing this weekend.

③ Michael is able to fix the radio.

④ Are you going to buy a new dress?

⑤ We shouldn't throw trash on the street.

10 다음 일기 예보를 보고 내용과 일치하면 T(true), 일치하지 않으면 F(false)에 ○ 표시하시오.

MON	TUE	WED	THU	FRI
sunny	cloudy	rainy (60%)	rainy (95%)	sunny

1) On Monday and Friday it will not be sunny. (T / F)

2) It may be rainy on Wednesday. (T / F)

3) You should bring your umbrella on Thursday. (T / F)

서술형

[11-12] 다음 문장에서 틀린 부분을 찾아 바르게 고치시오.

11 She cannot to be a famous singer.

(   ) → (   )

12 Benjamin should helps his mom this Sunday.

(   ) → (   )

서술형 NEW 내신 기출

13 주어진 말을 바르게 배열하여 문장을 완성하고 해석하시오.

(to, to, I, the park, would, go, like).

→ _____

→ _____

[14-16] 다음 밑줄 친 부분의 뜻이 나머지와 다른 것을 고르시오.

14 ① She <u>may</u> be a lawyer.

② The plane <u>may</u> arrive late.

③ The weather <u>may</u> be fine.

④ Nicole <u>may</u> win the contest.

⑤ You <u>may</u> stay here if you want.

15 ① I <u>must</u> read this textbook.

② You <u>must</u> clean your room.

③ They <u>must</u> bring their passports.

④ My sister <u>must</u> come back by 9 p.m.

⑤ He doesn't look well. He <u>must</u> be sick.

16 ① He <u>can</u> drive a car.

② I <u>can</u> climb the tree.

③ <u>Can</u> I go to the concert?

④ She <u>can</u> write an essay in English.

⑤ <u>Can</u> you remember her brother's name?

[17-18] 우리말과 뜻이 같도록 주어진 말을 사용하여 문장을 완성하시오.

17 그는 곧 이사 갈 것이다. (move)

→ _____ _____ _____ _____ _____ soon.

18 너는 물을 낭비해서는 안 된다. (waste)

→ _____ _____ _____ _____ water.

19 다음 중 어법상 옳은 것은 모두 몇 개인가?

> ⓐ Ava has to think about it.
> ⓑ He will be going to marry her.
> ⓒ Could you close the window?
> ⓓ The ice show must be exciting.
> ⓔ The patient may not to die.

① 1개   ② 2개   ③ 3개
④ 4개   ⑤ 5개

20 다음 중 대화가 <u>어색한</u> 것은?

① A: May I park here?
   B: Yes, you may.

② A: Can you see those small letters?
   B: No, I can't.

③ A: Will you go shopping with me?
   B: No, I won't.

④ A: Are you going to see your friends?
   B: Yes, I am.

⑤ A: Do I have to return this book now?
   B: No, you must not.

21 다음 우리말을 영어로 바르게 옮긴 것은?

> 오늘 눈이 오지 않을지도 모른다.

① It cannot snow today.
② It not may snow today.
③ It may not snow today.
④ It not must snow today.
⑤ It must not snow today.

[22-24] 다음 그림을 보고 조동사와 주어진 말을 사용하여 문장을 완성하시오.

22

You _____ _____ _____ here. (swim)

23

You _____ _____ _____ on the grass. (walk)

24

You _____ _____ here. (fish)

CHAPTER

06

의문사가 있는 의문문

의문사 who, what, which

A

의문사

- '누가', '무엇을', '언제', '어디서', '왜', '어떻게'를 물을 때 쓰는 말이다.
- 의문사가 있는 의문문의 어순은 『의문사+동사[be동사/조동사/do[did]]+주어 ...?』이며, 대답은 yes나 no로 하지 않는다.

1 who: '누구', '누가', '누구를'의 뜻으로, 사람에 관해 물을 때 쓴다.

A: **Who** made that soup?

B: I did. / I made it.

A: **Who(m)** did you meet yesterday?

B: (I met) My friend.

> **Tip 주의!** who의 목적격은 whom이나 who를 쓴다.

2 what: '무엇이', '무엇을'의 뜻으로, 사물이나 사건에 관해 물을 때 쓴다.

What is your dream job?

What do you do in your free time?

> **Tip 주의!** What do you think?: '어떻게 생각하니?'

3 which: '어느 것이', '어느 것을'의 뜻으로, 사물에 관해 물을 때 쓴다.

Which is the best idea?

Which do you want, pizza or pasta?

> **Tip 주의!** 정해지지 않은 대상에 대한 선택을 물을 때는 what을 쓰지만 정해진 범위 안에서의 선택을 물을 때는 which를 쓴다.
> **What** is your favorite color?
> **Which** color do you like better, pink or sky blue?

✓ Grammar UP

1 의문사가 주어일 때 3인칭 단수 취급한다.

Who **wants** this chocolate?

What **is** happening now?

2 의문형용사 what/which: 명사 앞에 위치하여 '어느', '어떤', '무슨', '몇' 등의 뜻을 나타낸다.

What *time* do you go home?

Which *movie* did you watch yesterday?

SPEED CHECK

빈칸에 알맞은 말을 고르시오.

1 _____ washed my car? – Sarah did.

① Who   ② What   ③ Which   ④ Why   ⑤ Whom

2 _____ did you do last weekend? – I went to the park.

① Who   ② What   ③ Which   ④ Why   ⑤ Whom

PRACTICE TEST

A ( ) 안에서 알맞은 말을 고르시오.

1 A: (Who / What) did he say?
B: He said "Thank you."

2 A: (Who / Which) do you want, beef or seafood?
B: I want the beef.

3 A: (What / Which) time do you go to bed?
B: Around 11 p.m.

4 A: Who (has / have) brothers or sisters?
B: Ben has a sister.

A
beef 몡 소고기
seafood 몡 해산물
around 뮌 약, …쯤

B 우리말과 뜻이 같도록 주어진 말을 바르게 배열하시오.

1 Erin은 어제 무엇을 했니? (did, what, Erin, do)
_____ yesterday?

2 그는 오늘 어느 수업이 있니? (have, class, he, which, does)
_____ today?

3 누가 거실을 청소했니? (cleaned, the living room, who)
_____

B
class 몡 학급; *수업
living room 거실

C 우리말과 뜻이 같도록 주어진 말을 사용하여 문장을 완성하시오.

1 누가 그 그림을 그렸니? (draw)
_____ _____ the picture?

2 너는 부모님을 위해 무엇을 샀니? (buy)
_____ _____ _____ for your parents?

3 너는 자동차와 자전거 중 어느 것이 더 좋니? (like better)
_____ _____ _____ _____, cars or bikes?

4 너는 사과와 배 중 어느 과일을 더 좋아하니? (fruit, prefer)
_____ _____ _____ _____, apples or pears?

C
draw 몡 그리다
(draw-drew)
fruit 몡 과일
prefer 몡 더 좋아하다,
　　　 선호하다
pear 몡 배

UNIT 2

의문사 when, where, why

1 when: '언제'의 뜻으로, 시간, 날짜 등을 물을 때 쓴다.

When is your final exam?

When will you go to Chicago?

When do you eat lunch?

 Tip 주의! 시간을 묻는 when은 what time으로 바꿔 쓸 수 있다.

When does the concert start?

(= What time)

2 where: '어디서', '어디에'의 뜻으로, 위치, 장소 등을 물을 때 쓴다.

Where are my socks?

Where did you get this coupon?

Where will you meet Mandy?

3 why: '왜'의 뜻으로, 원인, 이유 등을 물을 때 쓴다. 주로 because로 대답한다.

A: **Why** were you late for school?

B: **Because** I got up late.

A: **Why** did she call you?

B: **Because** she had a question about our homework.

 Grammar UP 의문사 why를 사용한 주요 표현

1 『**Why don't you + 동사원형 ...?**』: '···하는 것이 어때?'의 뜻으로, 상대방에게 권유할 때 쓴다.

Why don't you take a break? You look tired.

2 『**Why don't we + 동사원형 ...?**』: '우리 ···하지 않을래?'의 뜻으로, 『Let's + 동사원형 .....』과 비슷한 제안의 표현이다.

Why don't we go snowboarding?

SPEED CHECK

빈칸에 알맞은 말을 고르시오.

1 _____ do you study English? – Because it is useful.

① Who　　　　② What　　　　③ When　　　　④ Where　　　　⑤ Why

2 _____ did you buy these clothes? – At the new shopping mall.

① Who　　　　② Which　　　　③ When　　　　④ Where　　　　⑤ Why

3 _____ is the next meeting? – At 4 o'clock tomorrow afternoon.

① Who　　　　② Which　　　　③ When　　　　④ Where　　　　⑤ Why

PRACTICE TEST

정답 및 해설 p.15

A 빈칸에 알맞은 의문사를 쓰시오.

1 A: _____ did you hurt your arm?
B: Last Tuesday.

2 A: _____ did he miss class?
B: Because he was sick.

3 A: _____ did you lose your purse?
B: Maybe at the park.

B 다음 질문에 알맞은 대답을 보기에서 고르시오.

| 보기 | ① In Gangnam.   ② Because I had a cold.   ③ About 7 a.m.

1 Why did you go to the doctor's office?
2 What time do you usually get up?
3 Where did you see the musical?

C 우리말과 뜻이 같도록 주어진 말을 사용하여 문장을 완성하시오.

1 너는 어디서 그 열쇠를 찾았니? (find)
_____ _____ _____ _____ the key?

2 그 가게는 몇 시에 여니? (the store)
_____ _____ _____ _____ _____ open?

3 너는 왜 이 노래를 골랐니? (choose)
_____ _____ _____ _____ this song?

4 우리 캠핑 가지 않을래? (go camping)
_____ _____ _____ _____ ?

5 그녀는 언제 여기에 도착했니? (arrive)
_____ _____ _____ _____ here?

A
hurt one's arm
팔을 다치다
miss (동) 놓치다, 빼먹다
lose (동) 잃어버리다,
        분실하다
purse (명) 지갑

B
have a cold
감기에 걸리다
doctor's office 병원
usually (부) 대개
get up 일어나다

C
choose (동) 고르다,
        선택하다
go camping 캠핑 가다

의문사 how

1 how

1) '어떤', '어떻게'의 뜻으로, 상태, 수단, 방법 등을 물을 때 쓴다.

A: **How** are you today?
B: I'm great.

A: **How** do you get to work?
B: By bus.

2) 『**how＋형용사/부사**』: '얼마나 …한/하게'

- How old …?: '몇 살', '얼마나 오래된'
- How tall …?: '얼마나 높은', '얼마나 키가 큰'
- How long …?: '얼마나 오랫동안', '얼마나 긴'
- How often …?: '얼마나 자주'
- 『How many＋셀 수 있는 명사의 복수형 …?』: '얼마나 많은 (수)'
- 『How much＋셀 수 없는 명사 …?』: '얼마나 많은 (양)'

How old is your daughter? – She's 14 years old.
How tall is that model? – She's 180 cm tall.
How long were you in New York? – About 10 days.
How often do you go to the hair salon? – Once a month.
How many *friends* does Brian have?
How much *water* do you need?

✅ **Grammar UP** 의문사 how를 사용한 주요 표현: 『How[What] about＋명사/v-ing …?』 '…(하는 것)은 어때?' (제안)
『Why don't we＋동사원형 …?』이나 『Let's＋동사원형 …..』으로 바꿔 쓸 수 있다.
A: **How[What] about** *taking* a break? / **Why don't we** *take* a break? / **Let's** *take* a break.
B: That sounds good.

SPEED CHECK

빈칸에 알맞은 말을 고르시오.

1 _____ did you pass the test? – I practiced a lot.

① How　　　　② Where　　　　③ What　　　　④ When　　　　⑤ Why

2 How _____ did James play the game? – For about two hours.

① often　　　　② tall　　　　③ long　　　　④ old　　　　⑤ many

3 How _____ people are there in your family? – There are five.

① old　　　　② much　　　　③ many　　　　④ often　　　　⑤ long

PRACTICE TEST

정답 및 해설 p.16

A 다음 밑줄 친 부분을 어법에 맞게 고치시오.

1 <u>How many money</u> does she have?

2 <u>How much hours</u> do you sleep in a day?

3 How about <u>take a walk</u>?

4 A: <u>How tall</u> are you?
   B: I'm 7 years old.

5 A: <u>How long</u> is your brother?
   B: He's 150 cm tall.

B 다음 빈칸에 알맞은 말을 쓰시오.

1 A: _____ do you exercise?
   B: Almost every day.

2 A: _____ did she stay here?
   B: About a week.

3 A: _____ cups of coffee do you drink a day?
   B: Three cups.

4 A: _____ sugar did you put in your tea?
   B: I didn't put any sugar in it.

C 우리말과 뜻이 같도록 주어진 말을 사용하여 문장을 완성하시오.

1 Helen은 과학 공부를 어떻게 하니? (study)
   _____ _____ _____ _____ science?

2 너의 프랑스로의 여행은 어땠니? (trip)
   _____ _____ _____ to France?

3 음식점에 아이들이 몇 명 있니? (children)
   _____ _____ _____ are there in the restaurant?

4 저녁으로 피자를 먹는 게 어때? (have pizza)
   _____ _____ _____ _____ for dinner?

A
take a walk 산책하다

B
almost ⊕ 거의

C
trip ⑲ 여행
restaurant ⑲ 음식점, 식당

REVIEW TEST

[01-03] 다음 빈칸에 들어갈 수 있는 말을 고르시오.

01

> A: _____ is your birthday?
> B: It's March 11th.

① How   ② Why
③ What   ④ When
⑤ Where

02

> A: How _____ does he cook for his family?
> B: About twice a week.

① old   ② long
③ much   ④ often
⑤ far

03

> A: _____ size do you want, small or medium?
> B: I'd like a small size.

① How   ② Who
③ Which   ④ Where
⑤ When

04 다음 밑줄 친 부분 중 어법상 틀린 것은?

① <u>Who is</u> that girl at the door?
② <u>What do</u> Anna and Jake do?
③ <u>Why do</u> you keep a diary every day?
④ <u>How much</u> books did you read during vacation?
⑤ <u>How about</u> going to the beach this weekend?

05 다음 중 빈칸에 들어갈 말이 나머지와 <u>다른</u> 것은?

① _____ tall is he?
② _____ are you from?
③ _____ did you solve the problem?
④ _____ many boys are there?
⑤ _____ far is it from London to Beijing?

NEW 내신 기출

06 주어진 문장과 의미가 같은 것을 2개 고르면?

> Let's take the subway to work.

① How about taking the subway to work?
② Why about taking the subway to work?
③ What about taking the subway to work?
④ Which about taking the subway to work?
⑤ Where about taking the subway to work?

07 다음 빈칸에 공통으로 들어갈 수 있는 것은?

> • _____ deep can you dive?
> • _____ did you fix the machine?
> • _____ high is the bird flying?

① What   ② Which
③ When   ④ How
⑤ Why

08 다음 대화의 빈칸에 들어갈 한 단어와 보기의 단어를 한 번씩만 사용하여 문장을 완성하시오.

> A: _____ is the weather in Paris?
> B: It's sunny.

| 보기 |
> to   do   school   often   walk   you

→ _____ ?

[11-12] 다음 문장에서 **틀린** 부분을 찾아 바르게 고치시오.

11 How many salt do you need in your soup?

(   ) → (   )

12 Why don't you going home now?

(   ) → (   )

[09-10] 다음 대화의 빈칸에 들어갈 수 있는 말을 고르시오.

09

> A: _____
> B: Because I stayed up late last night.

① What did you do?

② Why are you so tired?

③ When did you get up?

④ Why didn't you stay up late?

⑤ What time did you go to bed?

[13-14] 다음 빈칸에 들어갈 말을 바르게 짝지은 것을 고르시오.

13

> A: Excuse me. ___@___ am I?
> B: You're here on this map.
> A: Thank you. ___ⓑ___ way is the subway station?
> B: Just go down this street.

	ⓐ	ⓑ		ⓐ	ⓑ
①	Where	– Why	②	Which	– Where
③	Where	– Which	④	Which	– Why
⑤	When	– Which			

10

> A: Which do you prefer, apple juice or lemonade?
> B: _____

① I like apple juice better.

② That is my favorite juice.

③ I'm ready to order now.

④ He wants some lemonade.

⑤ No, I don't. I'm not thirsty.

14

> Ann: ___@___ is this on the 10,000 won bill?
> Jinsu: That is King Sejong the Great.
> Ann: ___ⓑ___ did he do?
> Jinsu: He invented Hangeul.

*bill 지폐

	ⓐ	ⓑ		ⓐ	ⓑ
①	Who	– When	②	How	– What
③	When	– Why	④	Who	– What
⑤	When	– Which			

15 다음 대화의 빈칸에 알맞은 말을 쓰시오.

> A: _____ ⓐ _____ do you live?
>
> B: I live in Yongsan.
>
> A: _____ ⓑ _____ do you get to school?
>
> B: By bus. How about you?
>
> A: I live near the school, so I just walk.
>
> B: _____ ⓒ _____ does it take?
>
> A: About 10 minutes.

16 다음 중 대화가 어색한 것을 모두 고르면?

① A: What countries did you visit?
　 B: I'm from America.

② A: What did you do yesterday?
　 B: I went to my grandparents' house.

③ A: Which dish did you choose?
　 B: I chose the chicken curry.

④ A: Where is the famous restaurant?
　 B: Because it's delicious.

⑤ A: Who plays the drums in your band?
　 B: Jacob does.

[17-19] 우리말과 뜻이 같도록 주어진 말을 사용하여 문장을 완성하시오.

17 너는 세상에서 누구를 가장 좋아하니? (like)

→ _____ _____ _____ _____ most in the world?

18 너는 바지와 구두 중 어느 것이 필요하니? (need)

→ _____ _____ _____ _____, pants or shoes?

19 너는 그 시험을 위해 얼마나 오랫동안 공부했니? (study)

→ _____ _____ _____ _____ _____ for the test?

20 다음 빈칸에 알맞은 말을 써넣어 대화를 완성하시오.

> A: _____ _____ do you drink milk?
>
> B: Once a day.

21 다음 초대장을 보고 대화를 완성하시오.

> *Come to the school dance party!*
> **Date**: May 15
> **Place**: Student Hall

Ian:　Hey, Tina. _____ is the dance party?

Tina: It's on May 15. Are you coming?

Ian:　Yes. _____ is it?

Tina: It's at the Student Hall. _____ _____ _____ go together?

Ian:　Sure.

CHAPTER

07

기타 의문문/
감탄문/명령문

부가 의문문

○ 부가 의문문은 평서문 뒤에 덧붙이는 간단한 의문문으로, 상대방에게 동의를 구하거나 확신할 수 없는 일을 확인할 때 사용한다.

1 부가 의문문 만드는 법

형태	긍정문 뒤에는 부정의 부가 의문문 부정문 뒤에는 긍정의 부가 의문문	You *live* in Paris, **don't** you? You *don't live* in Paris, **do** you?
주어	평서문의 주어 → 대명사	*Jane* is outgoing, isn't **she**? *Joe and Ann* aren't busy, are **they**?
동사	be동사 → be동사 조동사 → 조동사 일반동사 → do/does/did	Ralph *was* sick, **wasn't** he? He *will* help you, **won't** he? They *love* each other, **don't** they?
	시제: 평서문의 시제와 동일하게	They *came* late, **didn't** they?

2 부가 의문문에 대한 대답: 우리말 뜻에 관계없이 대답하는 내용이 긍정이면 yes, 부정이면 no로 답한다.

A: The news is shocking, **isn't it**?

B: **Yes, it is. / No, it isn't.**

✓ **Grammar UP** **명령문과 권유의 명령문의 부가 의문문**

1 명령문의 부가 의문문은 긍정 또는 부정에 관계없이 will you를 쓴다.

Show me your drawing, **will you**?

2 권유의 명령문의 부가 의문문은 긍정 또는 부정에 관계없이 shall we를 쓴다.

Let's go together, **shall we**?

SPEED CHECK

빈칸에 알맞은 말을 고르시오.

1 You won't lie to me, _____?

① will you   ② won't you   ③ don't you   ④ aren't you   ⑤ didn't you

2 Christine has a great smile, _____?

① didn't she   ② has she   ③ doesn't she   ④ does she   ⑤ did she

PRACTICE TEST

정답 및 해설 p.17

A ( ) 안에서 알맞은 말을 고르시오.

1 They don't like curry, (do / don't) they?

2 The musical was wonderful, (was / wasn't) it?

3 Jessie won first prize, (doesn't / didn't) she?

4 Brian can pass the test, (can't / doesn't) he?

5 Let's have lunch, (don't / shall) we?

6 Ms. Green doesn't teach history, (does / doesn't) she?

7 Turn on the light, (will / shall) you?

A
wonderful (형) 훌륭한,
　　　　　아주 멋진
win first prize
일등상을 타다
history (명) 역사
turn on …을 켜다

B 부가 의문문을 사용하여 다음 대화를 완성하시오.

1 A: The school cafeteria is crowded, _____ _____?
　 B: Yes, _____ _____.

2 A: Ashley will join the music club, _____ _____?
　 B: No, _____ _____.

3 A: You're not going to go to England, _____ _____?
　 B: Yes, _____ _____.

4 A: You can speak English, _____ _____?
　 B: No, _____ _____.

5 A: John and Aria aren't twins, _____ _____?
　 B: Yes, _____ _____.

B
cafeteria (명) 카페테리아,
　　　　　구내식당
crowded (형) 혼잡한
twin (명) 쌍둥이 (중의 한 명)

C 다음 밑줄 친 부분을 어법에 맞게 고치시오.

1 She is an early bird, is she?

2 Clean up the kitchen, shall you?

3 Let's go to the swimming pool, don't we?

4 You had a great trip, hadn't you?

5 He doesn't have much money, doesn't he?

6 Jack can't drive a car, can Jack?

C
early bird 아침형 인간
swimming pool 수영장
trip (명) 여행
drive (동) 운전하다

부정 의문문, 선택 의문문

A

부정 의문문

1 부정 의문문: '···이지/하지 않니?'의 뜻으로, 동사의 부정형으로 시작하는 의문문이다.

1) **be동사**: 『Isn't[Aren't]/Wasn't[Weren't]+주어 ...?』

Aren't you tired?

Isn't he your teacher?

2) **조동사**: 『Can't[Couldn't], Won't 등+주어 ...?』

Can't she remember you?

Won't you come back?

3) **일반동사**: 『Don't[Doesn't]/Didn't+주어 ...?』

Don't you miss him?

Didn't he have any pets?

2 부정 의문문의 대답: 우리말 뜻에 관계없이 대답하는 내용이 긍정이면 yes, 부정이면 no로 답한다.

A: **Isn't** she lovely?

B: **Yes**, she is. / **No**, she isn't.

B

선택 의문문

1 선택 의문문: or를 사용하여 한쪽의 선택을 요구하는 의문문이다.

1) 의문사가 없는 선택 의문문

Is this book interesting **or** boring?

2) 의문사 which가 있는 선택 의문문

Which do you like better, meat **or** vegetables?

2 선택 의문문의 대답: yes나 no로 답하지 않고, 제시된 것 중에서 하나를 선택하여 답하거나 Neither.('둘 다 아니야.') 또는 Both.('둘 다야.')로 답할 수 있다.

A: Do you want to go to *the shopping mall* **or** *the department store*?

B: **(I want to go to) The shopping mall. / Neither. / Both.**

SPEED CHECK

빈칸에 알맞은 말을 고르시오.

1 _____ this your fault?

① Don't   ② Which   ③ Didn't   ④ Won't   ⑤ Isn't

2 _____ you need sunglasses?

① Doesn't   ② Don't   ③ Which   ④ Aren't   ⑤ Can't

3 _____ does she play better, basketball or baseball?

① Aren't   ② Won't   ③ Can't   ④ Which   ⑤ Don't

PRACTICE TEST

정답 및 해설 p.18

A ( ) 안에서 알맞은 말을 고르시오.

1 (Isn't / Doesn't) it a lovely day?
2 (Aren't / Don't) you want butter for your toast?
3 (Weren't / Couldn't) you get up early this morning?
4 Will you leave tonight (and / or) tomorrow?
5 A: Did you meet Eva or Sandra?
   B: (Yes, I did. / I met Eva.)

A
lovely 혱 사랑스러운; *멋진
leave 통 떠나다

B 우리말과 뜻이 같도록 질문에 대한 대답을 쓰시오.

1 A: Don't you agree with me?
   B: _____, _____ _____. (응, 동의하지 않아.)

2 A: Isn't she your sister?
   B: _____, _____ _____. (응, 내 여동생이 아니야.)

3 A: Doesn't Fred like rap?
   B: _____, _____ _____. (아니, 그는 좋아해.)

4 A: Aren't they free tonight?
   B: _____, _____ _____. (아니, 그들은 한가해.)

B
agree with …에 동의하다
free 혱 자유로운; *한가한

C 우리말과 뜻이 같도록 주어진 말을 사용하여 문장을 완성하시오.

1 너는 우리와 함께 갈 수 없니? (join)
   _____ _____ _____ us?

2 Maria는 저녁 식사 후 그녀의 이를 닦지 않았니? (brush one's teeth)
   _____ _____ _____ _____ _____ after dinner?

3 너는 초밥과 스테이크 중에서 어느 것을 더 좋아하니? (sushi, steak)
   _____ do you like better, _____ _____ _____?

C
join 통 함께 하다[가다]
brush one's teeth
이를 닦다
sushi 혱 초밥

감탄문

A 감탄문: '참 …하구나!'의 뜻으로, 기쁨, 슬픔, 놀라움 등을 표현하는 문장이다.

B 감탄문의 종류

1 what으로 시작하는 감탄문: 「What(+a/an)+형용사+명사(+주어+동사)!」

What a great song (it is)!
(← It is a *very* great song.)
What a good friend (you are)!
(← You are a *very* good friend.)

> **Tip 주의!** 명사가 복수이거나 셀 수 없는 명사이면 부정관사 a/an을 쓰지 않는다.
> **What huge signs** (they are)!
> (← They are *very* huge signs.)
> **What sad news** (it was)!
> (← It was *very* sad news.)

2 how로 시작하는 감탄문: 「How+형용사/부사(+주어+동사)!」

How beautiful (it is)!
How delicious this cake is! (형용사)
(← This cake is *very* delicious.)
How fast time goes by! (부사)
(← Time goes by *very* fast.)

 Grammar UP how로 시작하는 감탄문과 의문문의 어순 비교

1 감탄문: 「How+형용사/부사+주어+동사!」
How old **this house is**!

2 의문문: 「How+형용사/부사+동사+주어?」
A: *How old* **is this house**?
B: It's 100 years old.

SPEED CHECK

빈칸에 알맞은 말을 고르시오.

1 _____ children they are!
① What good   ② How   ③ What a   ④ How good   ⑤ What the

2 _____ the concert was!
① What a   ② How   ③ What exciting
④ How exciting   ⑤ How an exciting

3 _____ book it is!
① What an interesting   ② How an interesting   ③ What interesting
④ How interesting   ⑤ What's interesting

PRACTICE TEST

정답 및 해설 p.18

A 다음 밑줄 친 부분을 어법에 맞게 고치시오.

1 How smart <u>is</u> she!

2 What <u>good a time</u> we had!

3 How <u>a lucky</u> woman she is!

4 What <u>a man polite</u> he is!

A
smart (형) 똑똑한
lucky (형) 운 좋은
polite (형) 예의 바른

B 다음 문장을 감탄문으로 바꿔 쓰시오.

1 It was a very boring film.

→ What _____ _____ _____ _____ _____!

2 This smartphone is very expensive.

→ How _____ _____ _____ _____!

3 Tim bought a very expensive pen.

→ What _____ _____ _____ _____ _____!

4 Tommy runs very fast.

→ How _____ _____ _____!

B
film (명) 영화
expensive (형) (값이) 비싼

C 우리말과 뜻이 같도록 주어진 말을 바르게 배열하여 감탄문을 완성하시오.

1 세상은 참 좁구나! (world, small, what, it, a, is)

_____

2 그 아기는 참 사랑스럽구나! (is, how, the baby, lovely)

_____

3 그녀는 참 완벽하게 노래하는구나! (perfectly, how, sings, she)

_____

4 그들은 참 인기 있는 여배우들이구나! (they, popular, what, are, actresses)

_____

C
perfectly (부) 완벽하게
actress (명) 여배우

명령문

A

명령문: 명령, 권유, 요구를 나타내는 문장으로, 보통 주어(you)를 생략하고 동사원형으로 시작한다.

B

명령문의 종류

1 긍정 명령문: '…해라'의 뜻으로, be동사는 be로, 일반동사는 동사원형으로 시작한다.

Close the window.

Be quiet, *please*. (= *Please* be quiet.)

> Tip 주의! 부탁이나 요청 등을 부드럽게 말할 때, 명령문 앞이나 뒤에 please를 쓴다.

2 부정 명령문: '…하지 마라'의 뜻으로, 『don't+동사원형』의 형태이다.

Don't be afraid.

Don't give up on your dreams.

3 『명령문+and ….』: '~해라, 그러면 …할 것이다'

『명령문+or ….』: '~해라, 그렇지 않으면 …할 것이다'

Get up now, **and** you will be able to catch the train.

Get up now, **or** you will be late.

4 권유의 명령문: 권유하거나 제안할 때 쓴다.

1) 『**let's**+동사원형』: '…하자'

Let's order a pizza for dinner.

Let's have a surprise party for Marie.

2) 『**let's not**+동사원형』: '…하지 말자'

Let's not be late for the meeting.

- 명령문에 대한 긍정의 답변: Okay. / Sure. / No problem. / All right. 등
- 권유의 명령문에 대한 긍정의 답변: Yes, let's. / Okay. / Sounds great. / That's a good idea. 등
- 권유의 명령문에 대한 부정의 답변: I'm sorry, but I can't. / No, let's not. 등

SPEED CHECK

빈칸에 알맞은 말을 고르시오.

1 Please don't _____ in line.

① to cut   ② cutting   ③ cut   ④ to cutting   ⑤ cuts

2 Put on your coat, _____ you will catch a cold.

① and   ② or   ③ so   ④ but   ⑤ that

PRACTICE TEST

정답 및 해설 p.19

A ( ) 안에서 알맞은 말을 고르시오.

1 Please (leave / leaves) me alone.
2 Let's (go / goes) out for lunch.
3 Study hard, (and / or) you can pass the exam.
4 Don't eat too much, (and / or) you will have a stomachache.

B 보기에서 알맞은 말을 골라 ( ) 안의 지시대로 문장을 완성하시오.

| 보기 |　　make noise　　drive　　turn off　　open　　take　　meet

(긍정 명령문이나 부정 명령문을 만들 것)

1 _____ _____ _____ in the library.
2 _____ _____ the TV. You need to do your homework now.
3 Please _____ _____ too fast. It's dangerous.

(let's를 사용할 것)

4 _____ _____ _____ a taxi. We're very close to the post office.
5 _____ _____ the window. The weather is so nice.
6 _____ _____ at the café. I'll wait for you at the school gate.

C 우리말과 뜻이 같도록 주어진 말을 사용하여 문장을 완성하시오.

1 창밖을 내다보지 마라. (look out)
　 _____ _____ _____ the window.

2 당신의 우산을 접어 주세요. (close, umbrella)
　 _____ _____ _____ , please.

3 네 음식을 다 먹어라, 그렇지 않으면 너는 나중에 배고파질 것이다. (finish)
　 _____ your food, _____ you'll get hungry later.

4 네 친구들에게 친절해라, 그러면 그들도 네게 친절할 것이다. (kind)
　 _____ _____ to your friends, _____ they will be nice to you, too.

A
leave A alone A를 내버려
두다, 혼자 있게 해 주다
go out for lunch
점심 먹으러 나가다
exam 몡 시험
stomachache 몡 복통

B
make noise 떠들다
take 동 잡다;
　　　*(탈것을) 타다
library 몡 도서관
dangerous 형 위험한
close 형 가까운
gate 몡 문, 정문

C
look out 내다보다
close 동 닫다; *접다
later 부 나중에

CHAPTER 07 기타 의문문/감탄문/명령문　73

REVIEW TEST

[01-02] 다음 빈칸에 들어갈 수 있는 말을 고르시오.

01

> Tim wants some cake, _____?

① is he

② wants he

③ does he

④ doesn't Tim

⑤ doesn't he

02

> _____ great your teacher is!

① What

② What a

③ How

④ He's

⑤ How a

NEW 내신 기출

03 다음 우리말을 영어로 옮겨 쓸 때 사용되지 <u>않는</u> 표현은?

> 규칙적으로 운동해라, 그러면 너는 건강해질 것이다.

① or

② will

③ become

④ exercise

⑤ regularly

서술형

04 다음 표를 보고 대화를 완성하시오.

Sandwich	Waffle	Soda	Coffee
$5	$6	$3	$4

Sam: I want a sandwich and a waffle. The total is $11, _____ _____?

Jake: Yes, it is. Do you want soda _____ coffee?

Sam: Soda, please.

05 두 문장의 뜻이 같도록 할 때 빈칸에 들어갈 수 있는 것은?

> That's a very big watermelon.
> → _____ watermelon that is!

① What a big

② How big

③ So big

④ It's a very big

⑤ What big

서술형

[06-07] 다음 문장에서 <u>틀린</u> 부분을 찾아 바르게 고치시오.

06 Play your song for us, do you?

(_____) → (_____)

07 What a high mountains they are!

(_____) → (_____)

서술형

08 주어진 말을 바르게 배열하여 문장을 완성하시오.

(late, school, be, not, for, let's).

→ _____

09 다음 빈칸에 공통으로 들어갈 수 있는 것은?

> • The river is very deep. _____ swim here.
> • The red light is on. _____ cross the street.

① Isn't   ② Can't

③ Don't   ④ Not

⑤ Be not

[10-11] 다음 빈칸에 들어갈 말을 바르게 짝지은 것을 고르시오.

10
> ⓐ It is a very touching movie.
> → _____ a touching movie it is!
> ⓑ She is very smart.
> → _____ smart she is!

	ⓐ	ⓑ		ⓐ	ⓑ
①	What	–	What	② How	– How
③	What	–	How	④ How	– What
⑤	What	–	Why		

11
> ⓐ We can't go on a picnic tomorrow, _____?
> ⓑ You cleaned your room, _____?

	ⓐ	ⓑ
①	are we	– did you
②	are we	– didn't you
③	can we	– did you
④	can we	– didn't you
⑤	can't we	– didn't you

12 다음 중 어법상 **틀린** 것은?

① Didn't we order five books?

② Please be quiet for a minute.

③ You love your family, don't you?

④ Hurry up, or you will miss the train.

⑤ Let's will get together this weekend.

서술형

[13-14] 우리말과 뜻이 같도록 대화를 완성하시오.

13 A: 영화 보러 가자.
B: Okay. Sounds great.
→ _____ _____ to the movies.

14 A: 너는 녹차와 아이스티 중에 어떤 것이 더 좋니?
B: I like green tea better.
→ _____ do you like better, green tea _____ iced tea?

서술형 NEW 내신 기출

15 우리말과 뜻이 같도록 주어진 철자로 시작하여 문장을 완성하시오.

너는 이 영화가 마음에 들지 않니?
→ D_____ y_____ l_____ t_____ m_____?

[16-17] 다음 밑줄 친 부분 중 어법상 옳은 것을 고르시오.

16 ① <u>Let's don't</u> go there.

② <u>How good friends</u> you have!

③ Paul doesn't eat meat, <u>does Paul</u>?

④ Don't run too fast, <u>or you will fall</u>.

⑤ <u>Didn't she had</u> a driver's license?

17
① Isn't my cat cute?
② How delicious are they!
③ Please don't worrying about me.
④ Kim had a plan yesterday, hadn't she?
⑤ What did you visit, the museum or the gallery?

18 다음 중 대화가 <u>어색한</u> 것은?

① A: Isn't she amazing?
B: Yes, she is.
② A: He is Mr. Porter, isn't he?
B: No, he isn't.
③ A: Don't use bad words again.
B: Okay, I won't.
④ A: Is she a scientist or a doctor?
B: No, she is a scientist.
⑤ A: Let's make pasta for dinner.
B: That's a good idea.

19 다음 중 어법상 옳은 것은 모두 몇 개인가?

ⓐ We'll be late, won't us?
ⓑ What a wonderful story!
ⓒ Please don't smoke here.
ⓓ Let's wash the dog, will you?
ⓔ Bring your passport, or you can't get on the plane.

① 1개   ② 2개   ③ 3개
④ 4개   ⑤ 5개

[20-21] 우리말과 뜻이 같도록 주어진 말을 사용하여 문장을 완성하시오.

20 너무 빠르게 운전하지 마. 항상 조심해. (drive, careful)
_____ _____ too fast. _____ _____ all the time.

21 너는 저 불빛을 볼 수가 없니? – 아니, 보여. (see)
_____ _____ _____ the light?
– _____, _____ _____.

[22-24] (A)와 (B)에서 알맞은 어구를 골라 문장을 완성하시오.

———(A)———
• will go to an audition
• didn't get a good grade
• are working at a restaurant

———(B)———
• did he?
• aren't you?
• won't she?

22 You _____, _____?

23 Justin _____, _____?

24 Grace _____, _____?

76

CHAPTER

08

동사의 종류

UNIT 1

감각동사 + 형용사

A

감각동사: feel, look, smell, sound, taste를 감각동사라고 하는데, 뒤에는 형용사를 쓴다.

B

감각동사의 종류

1 『feel+형용사』: '···하게 느끼다[느껴지다]', '(촉감이) ···하다'
I **feel thirsty**.
This sofa **feels soft**.

2 『look+형용사』: '···하게 보이다'
The child **looks happy**.
You **look pale**. Are you all right?

3 『smell+형용사』: '···한 냄새가 나다'
Her perfume **smells nice**.
The noodles **smelled spicy**.

4 『sound+형용사』: '···하게 들리다'
The music **sounded wonderful**.
Let's go out and take a walk. – That **sounds great**.

5 『taste+형용사』: '···한 맛이 나다'
This fruit **tastes strange**.
This *bibimbap* **tastes delicious**.

> 감각동사 다음에 부사를 쓰지 않도록 주의한다.
> The milk smells **bad**. (← The milk smells ~~badly~~.)

 『감각동사+like+명사』: '···와 같이 느끼다/보이다/냄새가 나다/들리다/맛이 나다'
The baby **looks like a doll**.
It **smells like an apple**.

SPEED CHECK

빈칸에 들어갈 수 <u>없는</u> 말을 고르시오.

1 I feel _____.
　① great　　　② sad　　　③ good　　　④ nicely　　　⑤ sick

2 It _____ great.
　① looks　　　② sounds　　　③ sees　　　④ smells　　　⑤ tastes

3 This orange tastes _____.
　① sweetly　　　② sour　　　③ good　　　④ bad　　　⑤ nice

PRACTICE TEST

정답 및 해설 p.20

A ( ) 안에서 알맞은 말을 고르시오.

1 The soccer player looks (strong / strongly).
2 The music sounds (beautiful / beautifully).
3 This paper feels (rough / roughly).
4 The muffin on the plate tastes (delicious / deliciously).
5 The roses in the vase smell (good / well).

A
rough 형 거친
muffin 명 머핀
plate 명 접시

B 보기에서 알맞은 말을 골라 빈칸에 쓰시오.

| 보기 | look   tastes   strange   smell   warm |

1 His story sounds _____. Is it true?
2 You _____ sad today. What's wrong?
3 These apples _____ sour. I don't want them.
4 The cake _____ very good. Did you make it?
5 The stove feels _____. Did you cook something?

B
stove 명 가스레인지

C 우리말과 뜻이 같도록 주어진 말을 사용하여 문장을 완성하시오.

1 너는 외롭다고 느끼지 않니? (lonely)
Don't you _____ _____?

2 그 파스타는 맛이 훌륭했다. (wonderful)
The pasta _____ _____.

3 그것은 나에게 공평하게 들리지 않는다. (fair)
It _____ _____ _____ to me.

4 그 실크 치마는 촉감이 부드럽다. (smooth)
The silk skirt _____ _____.

5 그들은 그 사진 속에서 화가 나 보인다. (angry)
_____ _____ _____ in the picture.

C
lonely 형 외로운
fair 형 공평한
smooth 형 부드러운
angry 형 화가 난
picture 명 그림; *사진

수여동사 + 간접목적어 + 직접목적어

○ 수여동사는 '…에게'(간접목적어), '…을'(직접목적어)에 해당하는 두 개의 목적어가 필요한 동사로, give, buy, teach, send, show, tell, pass, lend, make, write, bring, get 등이 있다.

1 수여동사가 있는 문장: 『주어 + 수여동사 + 간접목적어 + 직접목적어』

I **gave her a pretty dress**.
　수여동사 ┐　┌ 직접목적어
　　　　　간접목적어

Could you **lend me a pencil**?

2 간접목적어와 직접목적어의 어순 전환
　• 직접목적어를 동사 바로 뒤에 쓸 경우 『주어 + 수여동사 + 직접목적어 + to[for/of] + 간접목적어』의 어순으로 쓴다.
　• 대부분의 동사는 전치사 to를 쓰지만 for 또는 of를 쓰는 동사도 있다.

　1) **to를 쓰는 동사**: give, send, show, tell, teach, lend, write, bring, pass 등
　　She *showed* me a new app.
　　→ She *showed* a new app **to** me.

　2) **for를 쓰는 동사**: buy, make, get 등
　　He *made* me some cookies.
　　→ He *made* some cookies **for** me.

> **Tip 비교!** 『ask a favor/question of + 간접목적어』: 이 두 가지 경우에만 전치사 of를 쓴다.
> I *asked* my friend a favor.
> → I *asked* a favor **of** my friend.

SPEED CHECK

우리말과 뜻이 같도록 할 때 빈칸에 알맞은 말을 고르시오.

1 나는 나의 가장 친한 친구에게 크리스마스 선물을 주었다.
I gave a Christmas gift _____ my best friend.
① about　　② with　　③ to　　④ for　　⑤ of

2 나의 엄마는 나에게 새 컴퓨터를 사 주셨다.
My mom bought a new computer _____ me.
① about　　② on　　③ to　　④ for　　⑤ of

3 Ellen은 그에게 질문을 했다.
Ellen asked a question _____ him.
① about　　② with　　③ on　　④ for　　⑤ of

PRACTICE TEST

정답 및 해설 p.20

A 우리말과 뜻이 같도록 빈칸에 알맞은 말을 쓰시오.

1 Irene은 그녀에게 문자 메시지를 보냈다.

Irene sent a text message _____ her.

2 George는 그의 아들에게 파스타를 좀 만들어 주었다.

George made some pasta _____ his son.

3 그녀는 밸런타인데이에 그에게 초콜릿을 주었다.

She gave chocolates _____ him on Valentine's Day.

4 나의 아버지는 지난달에 나에게 기타를 사 주셨다.

My father bought a guitar _____ me last month.

B 두 문장의 뜻이 같도록 문장을 완성하시오.

1 I bought this sweater for you.

→ I bought _____ _____ _____.

2 Would you bring me some water?

→ Would you bring _____ _____ _____ _____?

3 My grandfather told me an old story.

→ My grandfather told _____ _____ _____ _____ _____.

4 We can make a toy for your daughter.

→ We can make _____ _____ _____ _____.

5 I showed the paintings to my art teacher.

→ I showed _____ _____ _____ _____ _____.

C 우리말과 뜻이 같도록 주어진 말을 사용하여 문장을 완성하시오.

1 제가 당신에게 부탁 하나 해도 될까요? (ask, a favor)

May I _____ _____ _____ _____?

2 내게 소금을 건네줄래? (pass, the salt)

Can you _____ _____ _____ _____?

3 제게 커피를 좀 주실 수 있나요? (get, some coffee)

Can you _____ _____ _____ _____, please?

4 Brown 씨는 우리에게 프랑스어를 가르쳐 주었다. (teach, French)

Mr. Brown _____ _____ _____ _____.

5 신문은 우리에게 유용한 정보를 준다. (give, useful information)

Newspapers _____ _____ _____ _____.

A
text message
문자 메시지

B
sweater ⑲ 스웨터
toy ⑲ 장난감
painting ⑲ 그림

C
useful ⑲ 유용한
information ⑲ 정보
newspaper ⑲ 신문

동사＋목적어＋목적격 보어

- 목적어 외에 목적어의 성질·상태를 보충 설명하는 목적격 보어가 필요한 동사가 있다.
- 목적격 보어로는 명사(구), 형용사(구), to부정사(구), 동사원형, 분사가 쓰인다.
- 목적격 보어가 있는 문장의 어순은 『주어＋동사＋목적어＋목적격 보어』이다.

1 『make, call 등＋목적어＋명사(구)』: '…을 ～로 만들다'/'…을 ～가 되게 하다', '…을 ～라고 부르다'
  The TV show **made** her **a big star**.
  Her friends **called** her **"Solomon."**

2 『keep, make, find 등＋목적어＋형용사(구)』: '…을 ～하게 유지하다', '…을 ～하게 만들다', '…가 ～인 것을 알게 되다'
  The blanket will **keep** you **warm**.
  Your smile **makes** me **happy**.

3 『want, expect, allow, ask, tell, order, advise 등＋목적어＋to부정사(구)』: '…가 ～하기를 원하다/기대하다/허락하다', '…에게 ～하라고 부탁하다/말하다/명령하다/충고하다'
  I **want** you **to spend** more time with me.
  She **ordered** me **to sit down**.

    > **Tip 주의!** help는 목적격 보어로 to부정사나 동사원형을 둘 다 쓸 수 있다.
    > My friends *helped* me **(to)** move.

4 사역동사와 지각동사
  1) 『사역동사(have/make/let)＋목적어＋동사원형』: '…가 ～하게 하다'
     She **made** us **work**.
  2) 『지각동사(see, watch, hear, feel 등)＋목적어＋동사원형/분사』: '…가 ～하는/하고 있는 것을 보다/듣다/느끼다'
     I **saw** him **run[running]**. (목적격 보어로 현재분사를 쓰면 진행의 의미가 강조됨)

SPEED CHECK

빈칸에 알맞은 말을 고르시오.

1 His words made me _____.
  ① sad   ② sadly   ③ to be sad   ④ sadness   ⑤ am sad

2 I asked my mom _____ noodles.
  ① cook   ② to cook   ③ cooks   ④ cooked   ⑤ cooking

PRACTICE TEST

정답 및 해설 p.21

A 다음 밑줄 친 부분을 어법에 맞게 고치시오.

1 He told me call later.
2 The prize made her very proudly.
3 I helped my mom finding the car keys.
4 The doctor ordered me stay at home.
5 Bella let him to watch TV all night.
6 Keep your body health.

A
prize 몡 상
proudly 뷰 자랑스럽게

B 보기에서 알맞은 말을 골라 필요시 어법에 맞게 바꿔 쓰시오. (단, 한 번씩만 쓸 것)

| 보기 | feel   be   chat   pass   drive

1 I saw her _____ with her friends.
2 He made me _____ comfortable.
3 I watched my aunt _____ a car.
4 His parents expected him _____ the audition.
5 Mr. Smith asked his children _____ polite.

B
chat 똥 이야기하다
comfortable 혱 편안한
audition 몡 오디션
polite 혱 예의 바른

C 우리말과 뜻이 같도록 주어진 말을 사용하여 문장을 완성하시오.

1 나는 그 책이 감동적이라는 것을 알게 되었다. (find, touching)
   I _____ _____ _____ _____.

2 나는 그가 노래를 부르는 것을 들었다. (hear, sing)
   I _____ _____ _____ a song.

3 그 학생들이 나를 학급 회장이 되게 했다. (make, class president)
   The students _____ _____ _____ _____.

4 나의 조부모님은 내가 배우가 되는 것을 원하지 않으신다. (want, be)
   My grandparents don't _____ _____ _____ _____ an actor.

5 그 박물관은 우리가 영상을 녹화하는 것을 허락했다. (allow, record)
   The museum _____ _____ _____ _____ the video.

C
touching 혱 감동적인
class president
학급 회장
actor 몡 배우
record 똥 기록하다;
          *녹음[녹화]하다

REVIEW TEST

[01-02] 다음 빈칸에 들어갈 수 있는 말을 고르시오.

01

I just had some bread, but I still feel _____.

① hungry
② hungrily
③ be hungry
④ to be hungry
⑤ being hungry

02

He _____ some difficult favors of me.

① gave
② sent
③ asked
④ brought
⑤ showed

03 다음 우리말을 영어로 바르게 옮긴 것은?

그 이야기는 모두를 초조하게 만들었다.

① The story made everyone nerve.
② The story made everyone nervous.
③ The story made everyone nervously.
④ The story made nervous everyone.
⑤ The story made nervously everyone.

서술형

[04-05] 우리말과 뜻이 같도록 주어진 말을 필요시 어법에 맞게 바꿔 쓰시오.

04 Mike는 그의 아들이 마당에서 놀도록 했다.
→ Mike let his son _____ in the yard. (play)

05 나는 그 농구 경기 동안 내 심장이 빨리 뛰는 것을 느꼈다.
→ I felt my heart _____ quickly during the basketball game. (beat)

06 다음 빈칸에 들어갈 수 <u>없는</u> 것은?

The soup smells _____.

① strange
② delicious
③ well
④ wonderful
⑤ bad

서술형

[07-08] 두 문장의 뜻이 같도록 문장을 완성하시오.

07 Mr. James gave me lots of advice.
→ Mr. James _____ _____ _____ _____
_____ _____.

08 I'll get you some ice.
→ I'll _____ _____ _____ _____ _____.

NEW 내신 기출

09 주어진 말을 어법에 맞게 배열할 때 네 번째 오는 말은?

(up, me, he, to, ordered, stand).

① up
② to
③ me
④ stand
⑤ ordered

[10-11] 다음 빈칸에 들어갈 말을 바르게 짝지은 것을 고르시오.

10

> ⓐ We watched Cory _____ soccer.
> ⓑ Jake expected his mother _____ him a cat.

	ⓐ	ⓑ		ⓐ	ⓑ
①	play	– buy	②	play	– buying
③	to play	– to buy	④	playing	– buying
⑤	playing	– to buy			

11

> ⓐ You look _____ . Let's take a break.
> ⓑ Can you pass the ketchup _____ me?

	ⓐ	ⓑ		ⓐ	ⓑ
①	tired	– to	②	tired	– for
③	tiredness	– to	④	tiredly	– to
⑤	tiredly	– for			

12 보기에서 알맞은 말을 골라 필요시 어법에 맞게 바꿔 쓰시오.

> | 보기 |
> smile   eat   bitter   to
> 'Angel'   satisfied

1) I tried the coffee. It tasted _____ .

2) I call my brother _____ . He makes me _____ .

3) I saw a monkey _____ a banana. I gave another banana _____ him. He looked _____ .

13 다음 중 빈칸에 들어갈 말이 나머지와 <u>다른</u> 것은?

① I told my secret _____ Rachael.
② Dan will lend his car _____ her.
③ The boy showed a note _____ Kate.
④ My dog brought the ball _____ me.
⑤ Serena got cookies _____ her friends.

14 우리말과 뜻이 같도록 주어진 말을 바르게 배열하시오.

우리는 그에게 인내심을 가지라고 부탁했다.

(be, him, we, asked, to)

→ _____ patient.

15 다음 조건에 맞게 문장을 써넣어 대화를 완성하시오.

> A: Hi, Jason! How was your day today?
> B: I was very busy. _____
> (Tom이 내가 그 차를 수리하게 했어.)

> | 조건 |
> • 우리말 뜻에 맞게 문장을 완성할 것
> • have, fix를 활용할 것
> • 6단어의 완전한 문장으로 쓸 것

16 다음 중 문장의 전환이 바르지 <u>않은</u> 것은?

① He wrote his wife a letter.
  → He wrote a letter to his wife.
② Jane told me her troubles.
  → Jane told her troubles of me.
③ Tommy sent me some flowers.
  → Tommy sent some flowers to me.
④ My father bought me a laptop.
  → My father bought a laptop for me.
⑤ Can you bring me a cup of coffee?
  → Can you bring a cup of coffee to me?

17 다음 중 어법상 틀린 것은?

① I gave him a call.

② I asked a favor of her.

③ Your plan sounds perfectly.

④ This food tastes terrible.

⑤ He made a purse for his girlfriend.

고난도

20 다음 중 어법상 옳은 것은 모두 몇 개인가?

ⓐ I got a free drink. I feel lucky.

ⓑ I heard him to cry on the bed.

ⓒ This chocolate cake tastes sweet.

ⓓ He's making a doghouse to our dogs.

ⓔ She advised Tony sees a doctor.

① 1개　　② 2개　　③ 3개

④ 4개　　⑤ 5개

고난도

18 다음 밑줄 친 부분의 쓰임이 나머지와 다른 것은?

① Your present made me happy.

② The TV show made me hungry.

③ His speech made people fall asleep.

④ My sister made Jake a birthday cake.

⑤ The bestseller made her a millionaire.

서술형

[21-23] 우리말과 뜻이 같도록 주어진 말을 사용하여 문장을 완성하시오.

21 나는 내 여동생을 Jen이라고 부른다. (call)

→ I _____ _____ _____ _____.

고난도

19 (A), (B), (C)의 각 네모 안에서 어법에 맞는 말을 골라 바르게 짝지은 것은?

My mom made me (A) read / to read the book. It didn't look (B) easy / easily , but I found it (C) interested / interesting .

	(A)	(B)	(C)
①	read	easily	interested
②	read	easy	interested
③	read	easy	interesting
④	to read	easily	interesting
⑤	to read	easy	interesting

22 Bella는 그녀의 방을 깨끗하게 유지하려고 노력한다. (keep, clean)

→ Bella tries to _____ _____ _____ _____.

23 그는 내가 떠나길 원하지 않았다. (want, leave)

→ He didn't _____ _____ _____ _____.

CHAPTER

09

to부정사와 동명사

to부정사의 명사적 용법

A

to부정사(to-v): 『to+동사원형』의 형태로 명사, 형용사, 부사 역할을 한다.

B

to부정사의 명사적 용법: 명사처럼 주어, 목적어, 보어로 쓰인다.

1 주어: '…하는 것은[이]'의 뜻으로, 3인칭 단수 취급한다. to부정사(구)가 주어일 때 보통 가주어 it을 쓰고 진주어인
to부정사(구)는 문장 뒤로 보낸다.

To study every day *is* wise.

→ **It** is wise **to study** every day.
가주어   진주어

2 목적어: '…하는 것을'의 뜻으로, 동사 want, need, decide, plan, hope, promise 등의 목적어로 쓰인다.

I *want* **to be** a lawyer.
We *hope* **to see** you again soon.

3 보어: '…하는 것(이다)'의 뜻으로, 주로 주격 보어로 쓰여 주어의 성질이나 상태를 나타낸다.

His goal is **to play** for the national soccer team.
My dream is **to live** by the ocean.

4 의문사+to부정사

- what to-v: '무엇을 …할지'
- who(m) to-v: '누가[누구를] …할지'
- how to-v: '어떻게 …할지', '…하는 방법'
- where to-v: '어디로[어디서] …할지'
- when to-v: '언제 …할지'

I don't know **what to eat** for lunch.
She decided **where to go** on her vacation.

 Tip 주의! to부정사의 부정: not/never to-v

My sister asked me **not to wear** her sunglasses.

SPEED CHECK

빈칸에 알맞은 말을 고르시오.

1 _____ is hard to say goodbye.

① This   ② It   ③ That   ④ He   ⑤ She

2 I plan _____ to Vietnam.

① go   ② to go   ③ goes   ④ went   ⑤ to goes

3 I taught my mom _____ a smartphone.

① use   ② used   ③ uses   ④ how to use   ⑤ what to use

PRACTICE TEST

정답 및 해설 p.22

A 다음 밑줄 친 부분을 어법에 맞게 고치시오.

1 It is scary <u>go</u> to the dentist.

2 Robin wants <u>buy</u> a new oven.

3 They didn't know <u>to how get</u> to the station.

4 My plan for Saturday is <u>stay</u> home all day.

5 Ms. Allan told us <u>to not make</u> noise in class.

A
scary ⑱ 무서운, 겁나는
go to the dentist
치과에 가다
station ⑲ 역
make noise
(시끄럽게) 떠들다

B 보기에서 알맞은 말을 골라 어법에 맞게 바꿔 쓰시오.

| 보기 | invite   get   make   watch |

1 I hope _____ an answer from you soon.

2 It's not easy _____ new friends.

3 She decided _____ the movie again.

4 Alex asked me whom _____ to the party.

B
invite ⑧ 초대하다

C 두 문장의 뜻이 같도록 문장을 완성하시오.

1 To help people in need is a good idea.

→ It _____.

2 To be honest with your friends is important.

→ It _____.

C
in need 어려움에 처한
honest ⑱ 정직한

D 우리말과 뜻이 같도록 주어진 말을 사용하여 문장을 완성하시오.

1 매일 운동하는 것이 나의 목표이다. (my goal, exercise)

It is _____ _____ _____ _____ every day.

2 그의 바람은 그 여배우를 만나는 것이다. (his wish, meet)

_____ _____ _____ _____ the actress.

3 나는 언제 질문을 해야 할지 몰랐다. (ask a question)

I didn't know _____ _____ _____ _____ _____.

4 Andy는 내게 앉지 말라고 말했다. (sit down)

Andy told me _____ _____ _____ _____.

D
goal ⑲ 목표
exercise ⑧ 운동하다
wish ⑲ 소망, 바람

to부정사의 형용사적 용법과 부사적 용법

A

to부정사의 형용사적 용법: '···하는', '···할'의 뜻으로, 형용사 역할을 하여 명사나 대명사를 뒤에서 수식한다.

I have *a lot of work* **to do**.

There are *many interesting clubs* **to join**.

> **Tip 주의!** 주의할 어순: 『-thing/-one/-body로 끝나는 대명사 + 형용사 + to-v』
> We need **someone kind to help** us.
> Would you like **something cold to drink**? – Yes, please.

B

to부정사의 부사적 용법: 목적, 감정의 원인 또는 결과 등을 나타내며 부사 역할을 한다.

1 목적: '···하기 위해', '···하러'

He went to the library **to borrow** a book.

> **Tip 주의!** 목적의 의미를 강조하는 in order to-v: Eric came here in order to learn Korean.

2 감정의 원인: 『감정을 나타내는 형용사(glad, happy, sad, sorry, pleased, surprised 등)+to-v』 '···해서[하니] ~한'

We're *glad* **to see** you.

I'm *sorry* **to hear** the news.

3 결과: '(···해서) ~하다'

My grandfather lived **to be** 100.

She grew up **to be** a great pianist.

✓ Grammar UP

1 『형용사/부사+enough to-v』: '···할 만큼 충분히 ~하다' (→ 『so+형용사/부사+that+주어+can』)

Mr. Johnson is rich **enough to buy** a yacht.

(→ Mr. Johnson is **so** rich **that** he **can buy** a yacht.)

2 『too+형용사/부사+to-v』: '너무 ···하여 ~할 수 없다', '~하기에 너무 ···하다'

(→ 『so+형용사/부사+that+주어+can't』)

I'm **too** tired **to go** there with you.

(→ I'm **so** tired **that** I **can't go** there with you.)

SPEED CHECK

빈칸에 알맞은 말을 고르시오.

1 She is not the kind of person _____ a promise.

① break   ② broke   ③ breaks   ④ broken   ⑤ to break

2 Dan couldn't find anything _____ on TV.

① to funny watch   ② to watch funny   ③ watches to funny

④ funny to watch   ⑤ funny to watching

3 One morning the actor awoke _____ himself famous.

① find   ② finding   ③ to find   ④ found   ⑤ to finding

PRACTICE TEST

정답 및 해설 p.23

A 다음 밑줄 친 부분을 어법에 맞게 고치시오.

1 It is time <u>finish</u> your homework.
2 Luke was <u>pleased be</u> with his girlfriend.
3 The students should find another person <u>asking</u>.
4 Do you have <u>anything interesting read</u> on the train?
5 We need <u>somebody to move strong</u> these boxes.

A
finish 图 마치다, 끝내다
strong 圈 힘이 센, 강한

B 두 문장의 뜻이 같도록 문장을 완성하시오.

1 I failed the test. So I was sad.
   → I was sad _____ _____ the test.
2 I have many shirts. I have to wash them.
   → I have many shirts _____ _____.
3 The movie is too scary. I can't watch it.
   → The movie is _____ scary _____ _____.
4 This bag is so big that it can hold many books.
   → This bag is big _____ _____ _____ many books.
5 He is too busy to go to Brad's birthday party.
   → He is _____ busy _____ he _____ go to Brad's birthday party.

B
fail 图 실패하다; *(시험에)
  떨어지다
hold 图 잡고 있다; *(사물을)
  담다

C 우리말과 뜻이 같도록 주어진 말을 사용하여 문장을 완성하시오.

1 그녀는 프라하의 아름다움을 보고 놀랐다. (surprised, see)
   She was _____ _____ _____ the beauty of Prague.
2 Aaron은 그녀를 행복하게 해 주기 위해 Maggie에게 꽃을 좀 보냈다. (make, happy)
   Aaron sent Maggie some flowers _____ _____ _____ _____.
3 우리는 이야기할 것들이 많이 있다. (many things, talk about)
   We have _____ _____ _____ _____ _____.
4 Sally는 그녀의 딸을 돌봐 줄 좋은 사람을 원한다. (someone, nice, look after)
   Sally wants _____ _____ _____ _____ _____ her daughter.
5 그는 경주에서 우승할 만큼 빠르게 달렸다. (fast, win)
   He ran _____ _____ _____ _____ the race.

C
beauty 圆 아름다움
talk about
  …에 대해 이야기하다
look after …을 돌보다
race 圆 경주

UNIT 3 동명사

A 동명사(v-ing): 『동사원형＋-ing』의 형태로, 명사처럼 주어, 목적어 또는 보어로 쓰인다.

B **동명사의 역할**

1 주어: '…하는 것은[이]'의 뜻으로, 3인칭 단수 취급한다.

Taking pictures *is* very fun.
Making a study plan *is* important.

2 목적어: '…하는 것(을)'의 뜻으로, 동사나 전치사의 목적어로 쓰인다.

1) **동사의 목적어**: enjoy, finish, mind, avoid, stop, quit, give up 등의 목적어로 쓰인다.

Jay *finished* **writing** his report.

 동사 begin, start, love, like 등은 목적어로 동명사와 to부정사 둘 다 쓸 수 있다.
It suddenly *started* **raining[to rain]**.

2) **전치사의 목적어**

I'm proud *of* **winning** a gold medal.
I'm tired *of* **eating** cereal for breakfast.

3 보어: '…하는 것(이다)'의 뜻으로, 주격 보어로 쓰여 주어의 성질이나 상태를 나타낸다.

Carl's hobby is **collecting** foreign coins.
Ali's job is **making** movies.

 동명사의 부정: not/never v-ing
I'm sorry for **not telling** you the truth.
Never making mistakes is impossible.

C **자주 쓰이는 동명사 표현**

- go v-ing: '…하러 가다'
- keep v-ing: '계속 …하다'
- be busy v-ing: '…하느라 바쁘다'
- feel like v-ing: '…하고 싶다'
- be worth v-ing: '…할 가치가 있다'

My family will **go camping** next weekend.
Hazel **was busy packing** her bag.

SPEED CHECK

밑줄 친 동명사가 주어, 목적어, 보어 중 어떤 역할을 하는지 쓰시오.

1 Aria is afraid of failing the test.
2 I stopped watching comedy shows.
3 My favorite activity is drawing cartoons.
4 Watching horror movies is scary.

PRACTICE TEST

A 보기에서 알맞은 말을 골라 어법에 맞게 바꿔 쓰시오. (단, 한 번씩만 쓸 것)

| 보기 | spend   fix   drink   surf   study

1 _____ time with family is important.
2 Chris gave up _____ coffee.
3 Tony's job is _____ smartphones.
4 Emily is interested in _____ law.
5 My friend goes _____ every summer.

B 다음 밑줄 친 부분을 어법에 맞게 고치시오.

1 Steve enjoys <u>to be</u> alone on weekends.
2 Would you mind <u>explain</u> that again?
3 Alison and Ben <u>were busy to make</u> dinner.
4 I kept <u>called</u> my sister, but she didn't answer.
5 My duty is <u>guide</u> people to the concert hall.
6 <u>Having not</u> breakfast is bad for you.

C 우리말과 뜻이 같도록 주어진 말을 사용하여 문장을 완성하시오.

1 Lauren은 소설 쓰는 것을 잘한다. (be good at, write)
   Lauren _____ _____ _____ _____ novels.

2 Joe는 내 질문에 대답하는 것을 피했다. (avoid, answer)
   Joe _____ _____ my question.

3 나는 오늘 밤에 외식하고 싶다. (feel, eat out)
   I _____ _____ _____ _____ tonight.

4 Max의 문제는 너무 늦게 일어나는 것이다. (get up)
   Max's problem _____ _____ _____ too late.

5 산책을 하는 것은 네 건강에 좋다. (take a walk)
   _____ _____ _____ is good for your health.

A
spend ⑧ (돈을) 쓰다;
        *(시간을) 보내다
fix ⑧ 고치다
surf ⑧ 서핑하다
law ⑲ 법, 법률

B
alone ⑱ 혼자의
Would you mind ...?
…해도 될까요?
explain ⑧ 설명하다
duty ⑲ 의무; *직무, 임무
guide ⑧ 안내하다

C
be good at …을 잘하다
novel ⑲ 소설
eat out 외식하다
be good for …에 좋다

REVIEW TEST

[01-02] 우리말과 뜻이 같도록 할 때 빈칸에 들어갈 수 있는 말을 고르시오.

01

> 그는 조깅을 하기 위해 아침 7시에 일어난다.
> → He gets up at 7 a.m. _____.

① goes jogging
② going jogging
③ to going jogging
④ to go jogging
⑤ went jogging

02

> Ann은 나에게 조언을 해 줄 만큼 충분히 친절했다.
> → Ann was _____ me some advice.

① too kind to give
② kind to give too
③ kind enough to give
④ enough to kind give
⑤ enough kind to give

서술형

[03-04] 다음 문장에서 틀린 부분을 찾아 바르게 고치시오.

03 I want my dad to quit smoke.

(_____) → (_____)

04 Do you have anything to wear warm?

(_____) → (_____)

[05-06] 다음 빈칸에 들어갈 수 있는 말을 고르시오.

05

> I'm sorry for _____ late.

① to be
② be
③ to being
④ being
⑤ was

06

> Can you teach me _____ to make a pancake?

① what
② how
③ why
④ which
⑤ whom

서술형

[07-08] 두 문장의 뜻이 같도록 문장을 완성하시오.

07 Don't watch TV all day. It is not good.

→ _____ is not good _____ _____ _____ all day.

08 Linda is so sick that she can't go to school.

→ Linda is _____ _____ _____ _____ to school.

NEW 내신 기출

09 우리말과 뜻이 같도록 어구를 배열할 때 필요한 단어로만 이루어진 것은?

> 나는 그에게 나를 따라오지 말라고 말했다.

① I, me, him, not, told, follow
② I, me, him, to, no, told, follow
③ I, me, him, to, not, told, follow
④ I, me, him, to, no, told, followed
⑤ I, me, him, to, not, told, followed

10 다음 빈칸에 들어갈 말을 바르게 짝지은 것은?

> ⓐ It's fun _____ window-shopping.
> ⓑ The man gave up _____ mountains.
> ⓒ _____ fruit is good for your skin.

	ⓐ		ⓑ		ⓒ
①	go	–	climbing	–	To eat
②	go	–	to climb	–	Eating
③	to go	–	climbing	–	Eat
④	to go	–	climbing	–	Eating
⑤	to go	–	to climb	–	To eat

11 다음 중 어법상 틀린 것은?

① It was nice to meet new people.
② She kept to dance on the stage.
③ I don't have enough time to exercise.
④ Children should avoid eating fast food.
⑤ Dan is looking for somebody to feed his cat.

12 다음 빈칸에 들어갈 수 없는 것은?

> My husband and I _____ to travel around the world.

① planned
② hoped
③ decided
④ enjoyed
⑤ wanted

13 다음 그림을 보고 주어진 말을 사용하여 대화를 완성하시오.

Ella: What do you want to do today?
Jack: I _____ _____ _____ _____ with my friends. (feel, play basketball)

14 다음 대화의 빈칸에 들어갈 수 있는 것은?

> A: Did you start your report?
> B: Not yet. I don't know _____ about.

① write
② where to write
③ writing
④ when to write
⑤ what to write

[15-16] 우리말과 뜻이 같도록 주어진 말을 사용하여 문장을 완성하시오.

15 헬멧을 쓰지 않는 것은 위험하다. (wear, a helmet)
→ _____ _____ _____ _____ is dangerous.

16 Tom은 시험 기간 동안 머리를 감지 않는 습관이 있다. (wash)
→ Tom has a habit of _____ _____ his hair during exam periods.

17 ① She likes <u>to sing</u> songs.

② It's bad <u>to eat</u> late at night.

③ Scott will go abroad <u>to study</u>.

④ <u>To break</u> a mirror is bad luck.

⑤ His dream is <u>to buy</u> a sports car.

18 ① Jason wouldn't stop <u>bothering</u> me.

② Lia is excited about <u>going</u> to Guam.

③ Her favorite exercise is <u>swimming</u>.

④ Thank you for <u>sending</u> me flowers.

⑤ Mia keeps <u>talking</u> about her friend.

20 다음 우리말을 영어로 옮길 때 네 번째 오는 말은?

> 베토벤은 57세까지 살았다.

① lived ② to ③ be

④ years ⑤ old

[21-22] 우리말과 뜻이 같도록 주어진 말을 사용하여 직업에 따른 각 인물에 대한 설명을 완성하시오.

21 Roy는 소방관이다. 그는 사람들을 돕는 것을 즐긴다.

(enjoy, help)

→ Roy is a firefighter. He _____ _____ people.

22 Sharon은 의사이다. 많은 사람들이 진찰을 받기 위해 그녀를 방문한다. (visit, get)

→ Sharon is a doctor. Many people _____ _____ _____ _____ _____ _____ a checkup.

19 다음 중 어법상 옳은 것을 바르게 짝지은 것은?

> ⓐ Her job was report the news.
>
> ⓑ He doesn't know what do first.
>
> ⓒ Thomas is tall enough to be a model.
>
> ⓓ That's wonderful to see the stars at night.
>
> ⓔ I'm scared of walking alone at night.

① ⓐ, ⓑ ② ⓒ, ⓔ ③ ⓐ, ⓑ, ⓒ

④ ⓑ, ⓒ, ⓓ ⑤ ⓒ, ⓓ, ⓔ

23 다음 대화에서 어법상 <u>틀린</u> 부분이 있는 문장을 찾아 바르게 고쳐 다시 쓰시오.

> A: ⓐ I want to make some cookies for my parents. ⓑ But I don't know how baking them.
>
> B: ⓒ Let me show you. ⓓ I learned to bake cookies last year.
>
> A: ⓔ Thanks a lot.

→ _____

CHAPTER

10

대명사

UNIT 1 재귀대명사, this/that, 비인칭 주어 it

A

재귀대명사: '··· 자신'의 뜻으로, 인칭대명사의 소유격 또는 목적격에 '-self[-selves]'를 붙여 만든다.

1 재귀 용법: 주어와 목적어가 같을 때 동사나 전치사의 목적어로 쓰인다. (생략 불가)

  1) **동사의 목적어:** May I *introduce* **myself** to you?

  2) **전치사의 목적어:** **He** is talking *to* **himself**.

2 강조 용법: '직접', '스스로'의 뜻으로, 주어나 목적어를 강조한다. (생략 가능)

  Andy **himself** wrote the story. (주어 강조)

  We talked with *the dancer* **herself**. (목적어 강조)

> **Tip 주의!** 재귀대명사를 포함한 표현
>
> | | | |
> |---|---|---|
> | • introduce oneself: '자기소개를 하다' | • dress oneself: '옷을 입다' | • burn oneself: '데다', '화상을 입다' |
> | • enjoy oneself: '즐거운 시간을 보내다' | • hurt oneself: '다치다' | • cut oneself: '베이다' |
> | • help oneself (to): '(···)을 마음껏 먹다' | • teach oneself: 자습[독학]하다 | • in itself: '본래', '그 자체가' |
> | • by oneself: '혼자서'; '혼자 힘으로' | • for oneself: '스스로'; '스스로를 위해' | |

B

this, that

1 this: '이것', '이 사람', '이 ···'의 뜻으로, 가까운 대상을 가리킬 때 쓰며 복수형은 these이다.

  This is my book. ('이것')

  These are my neighbors. ('이 사람들')

  This bag is mine. (명사 수식: '이 ···')

2 that: '저것', '저 사람', '저 ···'의 뜻으로, 먼 대상을 가리킬 때 쓰며 복수형은 those이다.

  Is **that** your English teacher? ('저 사람')

  Those are her dolls. ('저것들')

  I like **that** kind of movie. (명사 수식: '저 ···')

C

비인칭 주어 it

시간, 날짜, 때, 날씨, 계절, 거리, 명암, 온도 등을 나타낼 때 비인칭 주어 it을 쓴다. 이때 it은 '그것'이라고 해석하지 않는다.

What time is **it**? – **It**'s 5 o'clock. (시간)

What's the date? – **It**'s May 10th. (날짜)

SPEED CHECK

빈칸에 알맞은 말을 고르시오.

1 The knife is very sharp. Be careful, or you will cut _____.

  ① itself   ② herself   ③ himself   ④ myself   ⑤ yourself

2 _____ is warm and sunny today.

  ① This   ② That   ③ These   ④ It   ⑤ Itself

PRACTICE TEST

A

( ) 안에서 알맞은 말을 고르시오.

1 She calls (herself / themselves) a genius.

2 Did they enjoy (themself / themselves) at the beach?

3 We made our study plan (ourselves / myself).

4 I think of (me / myself) as a positive person.

5 (That / It) is very dark in here. I'll turn on the light.

6 (This / Her) is my music teacher, Ms. Murphy.

A
call A B A를 B라고 부르다
genius ⑲ 천재
think of A as B
A를 B라고 생각하다
positive ⑱ 긍정적인
person ⑲ 사람

B

자연스러운 대답이 되도록 빈칸에 알맞은 재귀대명사를 쓰시오.

1 Who drew this picture? – Susan drew it _____.

2 Who taught you Spanish? – I taught _____.

3 The food smells delicious. – Help _____!

4 Did you help Austin do his homework? – No. He did it _____.

B
draw ⑧ 그리다
(draw-drew)

C

우리말과 뜻이 같도록 주어진 말을 사용하여 문장을 완성하시오.

1 너는 너 자신을 믿어야 한다. (trust)
   You should _____ _____.

2 토요일 밤이다. 지금 밖에 비가 오고 있다. (rain)
   _____ is Saturday night. _____ _____ _____ outside now.

3 Dan과 나는 우리 스스로 감자들을 기르고 싶었다. (grow, potato)
   Dan and I wanted _____ _____ _____ _____.

4 저 호텔 보여? 우리는 저곳에 머물 거야. (hotel)
   Can you see _____ _____? We will stay there.

5 Chloe는 팔이 부러졌다. 그녀는 지금 자신을 씻을 수 없다. (wash)
   Chloe broke her arm. She cannot _____ _____ now.

C
trust ⑧ 믿다
grow ⑧ 기르다
(grow-grew)
break one's arm
팔이 부러지다

one, some, any

A

one

1 앞서 언급된 명사와 같은 종류이나 불특정한 사물을 나타낼 때

I lost my backpack. I have to buy **one**.
$$(= \text{a backpack})$$

Is there a bank near here? – Yes, there's **one** on the corner.
$$(= \text{a bank})$$

> **Tip 비교** it: 앞서 언급된 특정한 사물을 가리킬 때
> Where is *my cell phone*? – **It**'s on the desk.
> $$(= \text{The[Your] cell phone})$$

2 앞서 나온 명사를 받을 때

Anthony has three *cats*: a white **one** and two black **ones**.
$$(= \text{cat}) \qquad (= \text{cats})$$

3 일반인을 나타낼 때

One should do **one's** duty.

> **Tip 주의!** one의 소유격: one's / one의 목적격: one / one의 복수형: ones

B

some, any: '조금', '몇몇[약간]의'라는 뜻으로, 대명사나 형용사로 쓰인다.

1 some: 주로 긍정의 평서문, 권유의 뜻을 나타내는 의문문에 사용

I bought **some** nice tea. Will you have **some**?
There are **some** cups on the table.

2 any: 주로 부정의 평서문, 의문문에 사용

Do you have **any** vacation plans?
I do**n't** have **any** plants in my house. Do you have **any**?

> **Tip 주의!** not ... any: '전혀 … 않다'

> **Tip 주의!** some과 any는 형용사로 쓰일 때 셀 수 있는 명사와 셀 수 없는 명사 앞에 모두 올 수 있다.

SPEED CHECK

빈칸에 알맞은 말을 고르시오.

1 Is there a bookstore near our school? – Yes, there's _____ across the street.

① any   ② some   ③ it   ④ ones   ⑤ one

2 I bought _____ cheese at the supermarket.

① any   ② some   ③ it   ④ ones   ⑤ one

PRACTICE TEST

정답 및 해설 p.26

A ( ) 안에서 알맞은 말을 고르시오.

1 One should keep (one / one's) promises.
2 I need a taxi. Please call (one / it) for me.
3 Would you like to drink (some / any) juice?
4 I don't have (some / any) time this weekend.
5 My father bought me a dress. (It / One) is red.

A
keep one's promise
···의 약속을 지키다
call ⑧ 부르다; *(전화를 걸어) 오라고 하다
would like to-v
···하고 싶다

B one, ones, it 중 빈칸에 알맞은 것을 쓰시오.

1 _____ should not hit others.
2 Do you prefer blue jeans or black _____?
3 This is not my bag. Mine is the green _____.
4 Did you find your purse? – Yes, _____ was behind the sofa.
5 She has warm gloves. I want warm _____, too.

B
hit ⑧ 때리다, 치다
other ⑭ 다른 사람[것]
prefer ⑧ ···을 더 좋아하다, 선호하다
jeans ⑲ 《pl.》 청바지
purse ⑲ 지갑
behind ⑳ ··· 뒤에
glove ⑲ 장갑

C 다음 문장에서 틀린 부분을 찾아 바르게 고치시오.

1 Will you have any pizza?
2 There are any hot dogs at home.
3 I don't have a dictionary. Can I borrow it?
4 My mom made soup. My family liked one.

C
dictionary ⑲ 사전
borrow ⑧ 빌리다
soup ⑲ 수프

D 우리말과 뜻이 같도록 주어진 말을 사용하여 문장을 완성하시오.

1 나는 아침으로 사과 몇 개를 먹었다. (apples)
   I ate _____ _____ for breakfast.

2 그녀는 새 옷에 돈을 전혀 쓰지 않았다. (money)
   She didn't spend _____ _____ on new clothes.

3 너 목말라 보인다. 내가 너에게 물 좀 가져다줄까? (water)
   You look thirsty. Can I get you _____ _____?

4 나는 축구공 하나가 필요해. 내가 어디서 하나를 살 수 있을까? (buy)
   I need a soccer ball. Where can I _____ _____?

D
spend A on B
A를 B에 쓰다

REVIEW TEST

[01-02] 다음 빈칸에 들어갈 수 있는 말을 고르시오.

01

> The telephone is broken. We should buy a new _____.

① it
② one
③ itself
④ ones
⑤ them

02

> I saw Jamie's Bakery on this street. But I can't find _____ now.

① it
② its
③ one
④ oneself
⑤ itself

03 다음 밑줄 친 부분의 쓰임이 나머지와 다른 것은?

① We did it <u>ourselves</u>.
② Ms. Jones said to <u>herself</u>, "I'm lucky."
③ The child hid <u>himself</u> under the desk.
④ It is my birthday. I bought <u>myself</u> a present.
⑤ Bruno and Sam were looking at <u>themselves</u> in the mirror.

04 두 문장의 뜻이 같도록 문장을 완성하시오.

Jessica doesn't like to travel alone.

→ Jessica doesn't like to travel _____ _____.

[05-06] 다음 빈칸에 알맞은 말을 쓰시오.

05 I bought three roses: a white _____ and two red _____.

06 You didn't have _____ food today. Would you like _____ cake?

[07-08] 다음 그림을 보고 대화를 완성하시오.

07

A: Do you like _____ flower?
B: No. I like _____ over there.

08

A: What color shirt do you want?
B: I want _____ _____ _____.

09 다음 밑줄 친 부분 중 생략할 수 있는 것은?

① The door opened by <u>itself</u>.

② Sugar is not bad in <u>itself</u>.

③ Jenny taught <u>herself</u> Japanese.

④ Danny enjoyed <u>himself</u> last night.

⑤ My sister <u>herself</u> cleaned the house.

서술형　NEW　내신 기출

10 다음 조건에 맞게 문장을 써넣어 대화를 완성하시오.

A: All the food looks great!

B: Please go ahead. _____

(마음껏 드세요.)

A: Thank you.

─ 조건 ─

• 우리말 뜻에 맞게 문장을 완성할 것

• help를 활용할 것

• 2단어의 완전한 문장으로 쓸 것

[11-12] 다음 중 어법상 **틀린** 것을 모두 고르시오.

11 ① What day is it today?

② Are those people from China?

③ That baby is my cousin. She is cute.

④ This oranges smell bad. I don't want to eat them.

⑤ That is 2 km from the flower shop to the post office.

고난도

12 ① I'll tell the truth to her myself.

② Henry doesn't express him well.

③ Is there any paper on the desk?

④ You have to eat some more vegetables.

⑤ My brother is too young to cook dinner in himself.

[13-15] 다음 빈칸에 들어갈 말을 바르게 짝지은 것을 고르시오.

13

A: Do you have ___ⓐ___ questions?

B: Yes, I have ___ⓑ___. Could you help me?

　　ⓐ　　　ⓑ　　　　　　ⓐ　　　ⓑ

① any　– some　② some – any

③ any　– any　④ some – some

⑤ some – one

14

A: I don't know ___ⓐ___ good restaurants. Do you?

B: Well, why don't we have ___ⓑ___ Indian food? There's a good Indian restaurant nearby.

　　ⓐ　　　ⓑ　　　　　　ⓐ　　　ⓑ

① some – some　② some – any

③ any　– any　④ any　– some

⑤ one　– some

15

A: Mom, this cup on the table is dirty.

B: Just put ___ⓐ___ in the sink and find a clean ___ⓑ___ in the kitchen.

　　ⓐ　　　ⓑ　　　　　　ⓐ　　　ⓑ

① one　– one　② one – it

③ it　　– any　④ it　– one

⑤ some – one

16 다음 쿠폰을 보고 빈칸에 알맞은 말을 쓰시오.

Special Coupon

Do you need _____ books?
Visit our bookstore. You can buy _____
at a 50% discount.

* *This coupon can't be used on _____ sale items.*

17 다음 문장 (A)와 (B)에 대해 <u>잘못</u> 설명한 학생은?

(A) It's about 50 meters from here.
(B) Look at the puppy! It is so cute.

① 소민: (A)의 It은 '그것'이라고 해석해.

② 새봄: (A)의 It은 거리를 나타내는 비인칭 주어야.

③ 혜윤: It's autumn now.의 It은 (A)의 It과 쓰임이 같아.

④ 한빛: (B)의 It은 대명사야.

⑤ 시아: (B)의 It은 앞에 나온 the puppy를 가리켜.

[18-20] 다음 문장에서 <u>틀린</u> 부분을 찾아 바르게 고치시오.

18 Oneself should help poor people.

(   ) → (   )

19 That was very bright in the house.

(   ) → (   )

20 At the age of seven, children should dress yourself.

(   ) → (   )

21 다음 중 대화가 <u>어색한</u> 것은?

① A: Are there any problems?
  B: No, there aren't.

② A: Did you buy a new car?
  B: Yes. It is in my garage.

③ A: Wow! Those sneakers look great.
  B: Oh, I like those white ones.

④ A: What are you going to do?
  B: I'm going to eat some snacks.

⑤ A: Is there a café in this building?
  B: Yes, there's any on the first floor.

[22-24] 우리말과 뜻이 같도록 주어진 말을 사용하여 문장을 완성하시오.

22 울타리 위에 고양이 몇 마리가 있다. (cats)
→ There are _____ _____ on the fence.

23 Juliet, 우리에게 자기소개를 해 주시겠어요? (introduce)
→ Would you please _____ _____ to us, Juliet?

24 오늘은 11월 15일이다. (November 15)
→ _____ _____ _____ _____ today.

CHAPTER

11

형용사와 부사

형용사의 역할

A

형용사: 형용사는 명사/대명사를 앞이나 뒤에서 꾸며주거나 설명한다.

1 명사나 대명사를 꾸며줄 때

It is an **old** *castle*.

I listened to **beautiful** *music* at the beach.

> **Tip 주의!** -thing, -body, -one으로 끝나는 대명사는 형용사가 뒤에서 꾸며준다.
>
> There's **something wrong** with this printer.
>
> (← There's **wrong something** with this printer.)

2 명사나 대명사를 설명할 때: 주어나 목적어의 성질·상태를 보충 설명하는 보어로 쓰인다.

Ann is **smart** and **friendly**. (주격 보어)

I kept *the door* **open**. (목적격 보어)

B

수와 양을 나타내는 형용사

1 many, much, a lot of, lots of: '많은'의 뜻으로, 뒤에 오는 명사에 따라 달리 쓴다.

1) 『**many**+셀 수 있는 명사의 복수형』

Megan has **many** *shoes*.

2) 『**much**+셀 수 없는 명사』

Ryan doesn't want too **much** *salt* in his soup.

3) 『**a lot of/lots of**+셀 수 있는 명사의 복수형/셀 수 없는 명사』

I invited **a lot[lots] of** *people* to my party.

We had **a lot[lots] of** *fun* on our last vacation.

2 a few, few, a little, little: a few와 a little은 '조금 있는', '약간의'의 뜻이며 few와 little은 '거의 없는'의 뜻이다. 뒤에 오는 명사에 따라 달리 쓴다.

1) 『**a few/few**+셀 수 있는 명사의 복수형』

I need **a few** *tomatoes* to make some juice.

He is not a famous singer. **Few** *people* know his songs.

2) 『**a little/little**+셀 수 없는 명사』

I only have **a little** *coffee* in my cup. Can you get me some more?

There is **little** *rain* in the desert.

SPEED CHECK

빈칸에 알맞은 말을 고르시오.

1 I feel cold. Can I get _____ to drink?

① hot   ② hotness   ③ hotly something   ④ hot something   ⑤ something hot

2 We have to hurry. We have _____ time to catch our flight.

① a few   ② few   ③ many   ④ little   ⑤ much

PRACTICE TEST

정답 및 해설 p.27

A 보기에서 알맞은 말을 골라 빈칸에 쓰시오. (단, 한 번씩만 쓸 것)

| 보기 | interesting   brave   cold   salty   fast

1 She has a _____ car.

2 The soup is _____.

3 The ice made my juice _____.

4 I found this cartoon very _____.

5 Someone _____ rescued the cat from the tree.

B ( ) 안의 말 중 알맞은 것을 골라 빈칸에 쓰시오.

1 (many / much)

1) There are too _____ cars in Seoul.

2) I couldn't give my friend _____ help.

2 (few / little)

1) Some plants need _____ water to survive.

2) _____ soldiers came back from the war.

3 (a few / a little)

1) My brother put _____ butter on the bread.

2) I have _____ days to get some rest at home.

C 우리말과 뜻이 같도록 주어진 말을 사용하여 문장을 완성하시오.

1 그 노래는 그를 행복하게 만들었다. (make, happy)

The song _____ _____ _____.

2 우리는 오늘 중요한 회의가 있다. (important, meeting)

We have an _____ _____ today.

3 나는 Ella에게 유용한 것을 주고 싶다. (useful)

I'd like to give Ella _____ _____.

4 경찰은 그 도둑에게 많은 질문이 있다. (questions)

The police have _____ _____ _____ _____ for the thief.

5 우리 팀은 그 경기를 이길 희망이 거의 없었다. (hope)

My team had _____ _____ of winning the game.

부사의 역할

A

부사: 부사는 동사, 형용사, 다른 부사를 꾸며주거나 문장 전체를 꾸며준다.

We *walked* **slowly**. (동사를 꾸며줌)
Leo is **quite** *kind*. (형용사를 꾸며줌)
Olivia answered me **very** *kindly*. (부사를 꾸며줌)
Luckily, *he survived the accident*. (문장 전체를 꾸며줌)

B

부사의 형태

대부분의 부사	형용사+-ly	new-new**ly**, quick-quick**ly**, sure-sure**ly**, beautiful-beautiful**ly**, real-real**ly**, slow-slow**ly**, kind-kind**ly**, nice-nice**ly**, sad-sad**ly** 등
-y로 끝나는 형용사	y를 i로 고치고+-ly	easy-eas**ily**, happy-happ**ily**, lucky-luck**ily**, heavy-heav**ily** 등
형용사와 형태가 같은 부사	high('높은')-**high**('높게'), fast('빠른')-**fast**('빠르게'), early('이른')-**early**('일찍'), near('가까운')-**near**('가까이'), late('늦은')-**late**('늦게'), hard('딱딱한')-**hard**('열심히') 등
〈부사+-ly〉가 원래 부사와 뜻이 다른 경우	**high**('높게')-**highly**('매우'), **hard**('열심히')-**hardly**('거의 … 않다'), **late**('늦게')-**lately**('최근에'), **near**('가까이')-**nearly**('거의') 등

Roy solved the puzzle **quickly**.
She couldn't open the bottle **easily**.
Violet can jump **high**.
The project was **highly** successful.

C

빈도부사: 어떤 일이 얼마나 자주 일어나는지 나타내는 말로, be동사나 조동사 뒤 또는 일반동사 앞에 쓴다.

0%　　　　　　　　　　　　　　　　　　　　　　　　　　　　　100%

never　＜　seldom, rarely　＜　sometimes　＜　often　＜　usually　＜　always
'절대 … 않다'　　'거의 … 않다'　　　　'가끔'　　　'자주'　　　'대개', '보통'　　　'항상'

He *is* **often** late for work.
She **usually** *walks* to school.
I *will* **always** remember your advice.

SPEED CHECK

밑줄 친 부사가 꾸며주는 말에 ○ 표시하시오.

1 Joe came home <u>late</u> last night.
2 Spanish grammar is <u>quite</u> difficult.
3 <u>Suddenly</u>, the bird disappeared.

PRACTICE TEST

정답 및 해설 p.28

A

( ) 안에서 알맞은 말을 고르시오.

1 The woman sings very (beautiful / beautifully).
2 (Sad / Sadly), Ethan said goodbye to her.
3 I (careful / carefully) held the baby in my arms.
4 Do you (often see / see often) your grandparents?
5 Josh talked too (fast / fastly). I couldn't understand him.

B

다음 Peter의 일과표를 보고 보기에서 알맞은 말을 골라 문장을 완성하시오.

| 보기 | sometimes usually always |

	Mon	Tue	Wed	Thur	Fri
have breakfast	✓	✓	✓	✓	✓
play online games	✓				✓
read the news on the Internet	✓	✓		✓	✓

1 Peter _____ _____ _____.
2 Peter _____ _____ _____ _____.
3 Peter _____ _____ _____ on the Internet.

C

다음 문장에서 틀린 부분을 찾아 바르게 고치시오.

1 Last night, it snowed heavy.
2 The bird flies highly in the sky.
3 I always work hardly. I am a hard worker.
4 They got married, and they lived happy.
5 Someone pushed me on the street. I near fell.

A
carefully (부) 주의하여,
　　　　조심스럽게
hold (동) 잡고 있다, 안고
　　　　있다 (hold-held)
understand (동) 이해하다

C
hard worker
열심히 일하는 사람
get married 결혼하다
push (동) 밀다
fall (동) 넘어지다 (fall-fell)

비교 표현

A **원급:** 「as+형용사/부사의 원급+as」 '…만큼 ~한/하게'

Your hair is **as long as** Sue's hair.

George is **as gentle as** his father.

> **Tip 주의!** 원급 비교의 부정: 「not as[so] + 원급 + as」 '…만큼 ~하지는 않다'
>
> I was **not as[so] busy as** she was.

B **비교급:** 「형용사/부사의 비교급+than」 '…보다 더 ~한/하게'

He writes reports **better than** I do.

Health is **more important than** money.

> **Tip 주의!** even, much, a lot, far 등: 비교급 앞에서 비교급을 강조한다.
>
> Your friend is **much** *stronger than* you.

C **최상급:** 「the+형용사/부사의 최상급」 '가장 …한/하게'

What is **the biggest** country in Europe?

She has **the most beautiful** smile in the world.

> **Tip 주의!** 「one of the + 최상급 + 복수명사」: '가장 …한 것[사람]들 중 하나'
>
> Yuna Kim is **one of the greatest skaters** in the world.

D **비교급과 최상급을 만드는 방법**

비교 표현			원급	비교급	최상급
규칙 변화	대부분의 형용사/부사	＋-er/-est	long	long**er**	long**est**
	-e로 끝나는 형용사/부사	＋-r/-st	cute	cute**r**	cute**st**
	〈단모음＋단자음〉으로 끝나는 형용사/부사	자음을 한 번 더 쓰고 ＋-er/-est	big	big**ger**	big**gest**
	-y로 끝나는 형용사/부사	y를 i로 바꾸고 ＋-er/-est	easy	eas**ier**	eas**iest**
	-ful/-less/-ous 등으로 끝나는 2음절의 형용사/부사 또는 3음절 이상의 형용사/부사	more/most＋원급	beautiful	**more** beautiful	**most** beautiful
불규칙 변화			good/well	**better**	**best**
			bad	**worse**	**worst**
			many/much	**more**	**most**
			little	**less**	**least**

SPEED CHECK

빈칸에 알맞은 말을 고르시오.

1 The white backpack is _____ than the black one.

① nice   ② nicer   ③ more nicer   ④ the nicest   ⑤ most nice

2 He is one of the _____ soccer players in the world.

① good   ② best   ③ better   ④ goodest   ⑤ most good

PRACTICE TEST

정답 및 해설 p.29

A ( ) 안의 말을 알맞은 형태로 바꿔 최상급 문장을 완성하시오.

1 The Pacific Ocean is _____ _____ ocean on Earth. (large)

2 Susan is _____ _____ girl in my class. (funny)

3 Tomorrow will be _____ _____ day of the year. (hot)

4 What is _____ _____ _____ story in the world? (beautiful)

5 Skydiving was _____ _____ _____ experience of my life. (exciting)

A
the Pacific Ocean
태평양
funny (형) 재미있는
experience (명) 경험

B 보기에서 알맞은 말을 골라 필요시 어법에 맞게 바꿔 쓰시오. (단, 한 번씩만 쓸 것)

보기	bad well thin new

1 He is _____ than he was before.

2 It was _____ natural disaster in China.

3 Mina speaks English as _____ as a native speaker does.

4 Dan is one of _____ members of our band.

B
thin (형) 얇은; *마른
natural disaster 자연재해
native speaker 원어민

C 우리말과 뜻이 같도록 주어진 말을 사용하여 문장을 완성하시오.

1 누가 이 반에서 가장 빠르니? (fast)

_____ _____ _____ _____ in this class?

2 그 바닥은 얼음만큼 차다. (cold)

The floor is _____ _____ _____ ice.

3 Michael은 그의 여동생보다 더 수다스럽다. (talkative)

Michael is _____ _____ _____ his sister.

4 이것은 한국에서 가장 오래된 나무들 중 하나이다. (old)

This is _____ _____ _____ _____ _____ in Korea.

C
talkative (형) 수다스러운,
말이 많은

REVIEW TEST

01 다음 형용사 중 부사의 형태가 <u>틀린</u> 것은?

① slow – slowly

② early – earlily

③ lucky – luckily

④ amazing – amazingly

⑤ beautiful – beautifully

[02-03] 다음 빈칸에 들어갈 수 있는 말을 고르시오.

02

> It was snowing ＿＿＿＿＿ in New York today.

① heavy   ② heavier

③ heaviest   ④ heavily

⑤ with heavy

03

> My brother speaks Chinese ＿＿＿＿＿ than I do.

① better   ② good

③ well   ④ weller

⑤ as well

---

04 다음 중 빈칸에 들어갈 말이 나머지와 <u>다른</u> 것은?

① I can't wait longer ＿＿＿＿＿ an hour.

② He feels better ＿＿＿＿＿ he did last year.

③ My girlfriend eats more ＿＿＿＿＿ I do.

④ Sophia is two years older ＿＿＿＿＿ I.

⑤ Hillary sings as well ＿＿＿＿＿ Nathan.

서술형

[05-07] 다음 문장에서 <u>틀린</u> 부분을 찾아 바르게 고치시오.

05 I traveled to a little cities in Europe.

(   ) → (   )

06 I go often to Broadway to see musicals.

(   ) → (   )

07 What was one of the difficultiest decisions in your life?

(   ) → (   )

08 다음 빈칸에 들어갈 말을 바르게 짝지은 것은?

> ⓐ Canada is ＿＿＿＿＿ than the USA.
> ⓑ Jeju is the ＿＿＿＿＿ island in Korea.

	ⓐ	ⓑ
①	big	– large
②	biger	– largest
③	bigger	– largest
④	bigger	– most large
⑤	more big	– most large

NEW   내신기출

09 다음 빈칸에 공통으로 들어갈 수 있는 것은?

> Mr. Green has ＿＿＿＿＿ least amount of experience, but he is ＿＿＿＿＿ best teacher.

① a   ② as   ③ the

④ than   ⑤ most

10 다음 대화의 밑줄 친 부분 중 어법상 틀린 것은?

A: You don't ① look good. Are you okay?

B: I can't ② sleep well these days. I ③ am tired always.

A: Oh, that's ④ too bad. Why don't you take ⑤ a warm bath? It will help.

11 다음 그림을 보고 주어진 말을 사용하여 문장을 완성 하시오.

Leo   Miu

I have two cats, Leo and Miu. Miu is _____ _____ Leo. (small)

12 다음 중 어법상 틀린 것은?

① My mother drives a car well.

② Jack never breaks his promises.

③ This is the best car in our shop.

④ Prices are very highly in Tokyo.

⑤ Theater tickets are more expensive than movie tickets.

[13-15] 우리말과 뜻이 같도록 주어진 말을 사용하여 문 장을 완성하시오.

13 이 재킷은 저 코트만큼 따뜻하지는 않다. (warm)

→ This jacket is _____ _____ _____ _____ that coat.

14 스노보드 타기는 스키 타기보다 훨씬 더 재미있다. (interesting)

→ Snowboarding is _____ _____ _____ _____ _____ skiing.

15 책 몇 권을 살 약간의 돈을 받을 수 있을까요? (money)

→ Can I have _____ _____ _____ to buy some books?

16 다음 과목별 선호도를 나타낸 표의 내용과 일치하지 않는 것은?

Music	English	Art	Korean	Science
20%	40%	10%	15%	15%

① Art is not the most popular subject.

② Korean is more popular than art.

③ English is the most popular subject.

④ Science is not as popular as Korean.

⑤ The students like music better than Korean.

17 다음 중 어법상 옳은 것을 바르게 짝지은 것은?

> ⓐ I put a lot of fruit in my salad.
> ⓑ My arm is as long as Veronica's.
> ⓒ The thief took expensive everything.
> ⓓ Mark studies much harder than Ava.
> ⓔ Ian came to class lately this morning.

① ⓐ, ⓒ   ② ⓑ, ⓒ   ③ ⓐ, ⓑ, ⓓ

④ ⓐ, ⓓ, ⓔ   ⑤ ⓑ, ⓓ, ⓔ

[18-20] 보기에서 알맞은 말을 골라 빈칸에 쓰시오.

| 보기 |
| a few   much   little |

18 We met _____ tourists in Myeongdong.

19 The puppy ate _____ food. He must be sick.

20 The travel center doesn't have _____ information about Guam. I should search the Internet.

21 주어진 말을 바르게 배열하여 문장을 완성하고 해석하시오.

(sports, most, of, baseball, one, the, popular, is) in Korea.

→ _____ in Korea.

→ _____

22 다음 우리말을 영어로 바르게 옮긴 것은?

> 봄은 여름만큼 덥지는 않다.

① Summer is as hot as spring.

② Spring is not hot as summer.

③ Summer is not so hot as spring.

④ Spring is not as hot as summer.

⑤ Spring is as not hot as summer.

23 다음 빈칸에 들어갈 수 <u>없는</u> 것은?

> Jennifer makes _____ more money than Sam.

① much   ② even

③ a lot   ④ very

⑤ far

24 우리말과 뜻이 같도록 빈도부사와 주어진 말을 사용하여 문장을 완성하시오.

나는 가끔 나의 옛 친구들이 그립다. (miss)

→ I _____ _____ my old friends.

CHAPTER

12

전치사

시간의 전치사

전치사: 명사(구)나 목적격 대명사 앞에서 시간, 장소, 방법, 이유 등을 나타낸다. 한 전치사는 여러 가지 뜻으로 쓰일 수 있다.

시간의 전치사

1 in, on, at: '…에'

	쓰임	예
in	연도, 계절, 월, 하루의 때(오전, 오후)	**in** 2020, **in** winter, **in** May, **in** the morning
on	날짜, 요일, 특정한 날	**on** July 6, **on** Thursday, **on** Mother's Day
at	구체적인 시각, 하루의 때	**at** nine o'clock, **at** noon, **at** night

Pablo Picasso was born **in** 1881.
There is a big soccer match **on** April 17.
She left **at** five o'clock.

> **Tip 주의!** 시간이나 요일의 명사 앞에 this, that, next, last 등이 있으면 전치사 in, on, at을 쓰지 않는다.
> What did you do **last night**?
> (← What did you do **at last night**?)

2 around: '…쯤', '… 무렵'

I saw him **around** two months ago.
He arrived at the station **around** three o'clock.

3 before: '… 전에' / after: '… 후에'

We have to leave home **before** sunrise.
Let's go to the mall **after** class.

4 for, during: '… 동안'

1) 『for+숫자를 포함한 구체적인 기간』
   We're going to stay in Germany **for** *six days*.

2) 『during+특정한 때를 나타내는 명사』
   I had a cup of coffee **during** *the meeting*.

SPEED CHECK

빈칸에 알맞은 말을 고르시오.

1 The hair salon is closed _____ Mondays.

① in ② on ③ at ④ around ⑤ after

2 I took a shower _____ seven o'clock this morning.

① in ② on ③ at ④ to ⑤ for

PRACTICE TEST

정답 및 해설 p.30

A 다음 밑줄 친 부분을 어법에 맞게 고치시오.

1 The weather is very hot <u>on</u> August.
2 Don't talk on your phone <u>for</u> the movie.
3 The match starts <u>for</u> 11 a.m. <u>at</u> Saturday.
4 I met Chloe for the first time <u>at</u> Christmas Eve.
5 You can download the app for free <u>during</u> two hours only.

A
weather ⑲ 날씨
download
⑧ (데이터를) 내려받다
for free 무료로

B 보기에서 알맞은 전치사를 골라 문장을 완성하시오.

| 보기 | in   on   at   after   during   for |

1 They will go to the toy museum _____ May 5.
2 Maya went to India _____ 2017.
3 Fasten your seat belt _____ the flight.
4 Shall we meet _____ 10:30 at the bus stop?
5 She didn't eat sugar _____ two weeks.
6 She apologized to me _____ our fight.

B
fasten ⑧ 매다
seat belt 안전벨트
bus stop 버스 정류장
apologize ⑧ 사과하다
fight ⑲ 싸움, 다툼

C 우리말과 뜻이 같도록 주어진 말을 사용하여 문장을 완성하시오.

1 여름에는 비가 많이 내린다. (summer)

It rains a lot _____ _____.

2 정오 무렵에 저를 방문해 주세요. (noon)

Please visit me _____ _____.

3 점심 전에 손을 씻어라. (lunch)

Wash your hands _____ _____.

4 밤에 혼자 나가지 마라. (night)

Don't go out by yourself _____ _____.

C
noon ⑲ 정오, 낮 12시
wash ⑧ 씻다
by oneself 혼자

장소의 전치사

1 in, at, on

	의미와 쓰임	예
in	'… 안에', '…에(서)' (사물/건물의 내부, 도시, 국가 등의 비교적 넓은 장소)	**in** the box, **in** the room, **in** London, **in** Korea
at	'…에(서)' (비교적 좁은 장소나 지점)	**at** home, **at** a party, **at** school
on	'… 위에', '…에' (접촉해 있는 상태)	**on** the table, **on** the wall

Serena put the gift **in** the box.
He waited for her **at** the restaurant.
Don't walk **on** the grass.

2 near: '… 근처에' / next to: '… 옆에', '… 곁에'
Is there a market **near** your house?
The bathroom is **next to** the kitchen.

3 over: '… 위쪽에[으로]' (접촉해 있지 않은 상태) / under: '… 아래에[로]'
He kicked the ball **over** the roof.
The dog is sleeping **under** a tree.

4 behind: '… 뒤에' / in front of: '… 앞에'
Look at the moon **behind** the clouds.
She practiced dancing **in front of** the mirror.

5 across from: '… 맞은편에' (= opposite)
There's a café **across from** my house.
The baseball stadium is **across from** the park.

SPEED CHECK

빈칸에 알맞은 말을 고르시오.

1 The Chinese restaurant is _____ the fire station.
① from　　　　② in front　　　　③ on　　　　④ near　　　　⑤ for

2 Julie is washing her hair _____ the bathroom.
① in　　　　② on　　　　③ in front　　　　④ over　　　　⑤ under

3 My friends and I were lying _____ the ground.
① in　　　　② at　　　　③ to　　　　④ on　　　　⑤ opposite

PRACTICE TEST

정답 및 해설 p.31

A ( ) 안에서 알맞은 말을 고르시오.

1 The airplane flew (over / on) the city.
2 Is there a pharmacy (near / to) the hospital?
3 There's a library (across / in front) from the school.

B 다음 그림을 보고 빈칸에 알맞은 전치사를 쓰시오.

1 There is a table _____ the room.
2 I like the picture _____ the wall.
3 There is a light _____ the table.
4 My smartphone is _____ the table.
5 There is a rug _____ the floor.
6 There is a chair _____ the table.

C 우리말과 뜻이 같도록 주어진 말을 사용하여 문장을 완성하시오.

1 나의 삼촌은 젊었을 때 캐나다에 살았다. (Canada)
   My uncle lived _____ _____ during his youth.

2 방문객들은 종이에 그들의 이름을 적었다. (the paper)
   The visitors wrote their names _____ _____ _____.

3 Colin은 내 차 옆에 주차했다. (my car)
   Colin parked _____ _____ _____ _____.

4 Glenn이 바로 내 앞에 서 있었다. (me)
   Glenn was standing right _____ _____ _____.

A
fly ⑧ 날다 (fly-flew)
pharmacy ⑲ 약국

B
light ⑲ 전등
rug ⑲ 깔개, (작은) 카펫

C
youth ⑲ 젊음; *젊을 때
visitor ⑲ 방문객
right ⑨ 정확히, 바로, 꼭

기타 전치사

1 for: '…을 위해[한]' (목적); '…을 향해' (방향)
This letter is **for** Marie.
I left **for** Paris.

2 to: '…에', '…으로' (방향); '…에게' (대상)
You need to go **to** the meeting.
Did you speak **to** her?

3 between A and B: 'A와 B 사이에' (시간, 장소)
I'm free **between** 8 p.m. **and** 9 p.m. today.
Sweden is **between** Finland **and** Norway.

4 from: '…(로)부터' (시간, 장소, 출신) / from A to B: 'A부터 B까지' (시간, 장소)
Shane comes **from** Canada.
Riley works **from** 9 a.m. **to** 6 p.m.
How far is it **from** here **to** the park?

5 with: '…와 함께', '…을 가지고' / about: '…에 관해[한]' / of: '…의'
Can you play tennis **with** me?
The test was **about** grammar.
This is the end **of** the story.

> **Grammar UP** 동사와 전치사가 하나의 동사처럼 쓰이는 경우
> • look at('…을 보다'), look after('…을 돌보다'), listen to('…을 듣다'), wait for('…을 기다리다') 등
> Liam will **look after** his sick grandmother.
> Elsa is **listening to** music in her room.
> We **waited for** you all day long.

SPEED CHECK

빈칸에 알맞은 말을 고르시오.

1 She read a book _____ stars.
① about   ② with   ③ in   ④ from   ⑤ for

2 I'm usually busy _____ 2 p.m. and 5 p.m.
① on   ② for   ③ with   ④ across   ⑤ between

3 Matt will be in Singapore _____ this Friday to Sunday.
① from   ② for   ③ to   ④ about   ⑤ between

PRACTICE TEST

A ( ) 안에서 알맞은 말을 고르시오.

1 This swimming pool is (to / for) kids.
2 We looked (to / at) the old photos in the album.
3 Will you come to the concert (with / about) us?
4 Who won the soccer match between Korea (and / on) Japan?
5 The windows (of / from) this house are very big.

A
kid 명 아이, 어린이
concert 명 콘서트, 음악회

B 보기에서 알맞은 말을 골라 문장을 완성하시오.

| 보기 | to me   from my classmate   of the king's life
         and the post office   about your childhood

1 This is the story _____.
2 My family is very important _____.
3 Tell me _____.
4 I heard a secret _____.
5 The bookstore is between the bakery _____.

B
classmate 명 반 친구
post office 우체국
childhood 명 어린 시절
bakery 명 빵집, 제과점

C 우리말과 뜻이 같도록 주어진 말을 사용하여 문장을 완성하시오.

1 그녀는 그녀의 남자친구를 기다리고 있었다. (wait)
  She was _____ _____ her boyfriend.

2 여기서부터 우리는 걸어가야 한다. (here)
  _____ _____, we have to walk.

3 너는 머리부터 발가락까지 아름답다. (head, toe)
  You are beautiful _____ _____ _____ _____.

4 나는 내 여동생과 함께 우리 아빠를 위한 선물을 하나 샀다. (my dad)
  I bought a present _____ _____ _____ _____ my sister.

5 그는 한 마법사에 관한 이야기를 하나 썼다. 그는 그것을 그의 아들에게 읽어 주었다.
  (a wizard, son)
  He wrote a story _____ _____ _____. He read it _____ _____
  _____.

C
toe 명 발가락
present 명 선물
wizard 명 마법사
write 동 쓰다
(write-wrote)

REVIEW TEST

[01-02] 다음 빈칸에 들어갈 수 있는 말을 고르시오.

01

Sally's family usually travels _____ the spring.

① of   ② on   ③ about

④ in   ⑤ to

02

I want to have lunch _____ noon.

① in   ② on   ③ to

④ at   ⑤ between

NEW 내신 기출

03 다음 대화의 빈칸에 공통으로 들어갈 수 있는 것은?

- A: Where does he come _____?
  B: Canada, I believe.

- A: Where is your school?
  B: It is across _____ the stadium.

① in   ② at   ③ to

④ from   ⑤ near

서술형

04 다음 광고를 보고 보기에서 알맞은 말을 골라 ⓐ-ⓓ 에 쓰시오.

| 보기 |
| with   from   in   about   for   to |

We have many yoga classes.

Class A is ____ⓐ____ women ____ⓑ____ babies.
Class B is ____ⓐ____ office workers.
Our teachers are all ____ⓒ____ India.
You can ask them anything ____ⓓ____ yoga.

ⓐ _____   ⓑ _____   ⓒ _____   ⓓ _____

[05-06] 우리말과 뜻이 같도록 할 때 빈칸에 들어갈 수 있는 말을 고르시오.

05

출발 전에 다시 전화할게요.
→ I will call again _____ departure.

① for   ② next   ③ after

④ before   ⑤ around

06

나는 그 기차를 타려면 6시쯤에 일어나야 한다.
→ I have to get up _____ 6:00 to catch the train.

① in   ② around   ③ from

④ next to   ⑤ between

서술형

07 다음 지도를 보고 대화를 완성하시오.

A: Excuse me. Where's the bookstore?

B: Turn right _____ the bank. It's _____ the post office _____ the shoe store. You can't miss it.

A: Thank you!

122

[08-09] 다음 밑줄 친 부분 중 어법상 틀린 것을 고르시오.

08
① There is a park <u>near</u> the river.
② I lived <u>at</u> London when I was young.
③ They went on a picnic <u>on</u> Sunday.
④ His laptop was <u>on</u> the desk.
⑤ It takes about four hours <u>from</u> Seoul to Hong Kong by airplane.

09
① My house is <u>in front of</u> a church.
② Let's have dinner <u>before</u> the meeting.
③ Evie was born <u>in</u> January 7, 2002.
④ James traveled to Europe <u>with</u> his friends.
⑤ Questions <u>about</u> the law are difficult.

[10-11] 다음 빈칸에 공통으로 들어갈 수 있는 전치사를 쓰시오.

10
• Ron went back _____ his country.
• Don't tell this secret _____ anyone.

11
• I'm going on holiday _____ July.
• Some people are talking _____ the living room.

[12-14] 다음 학예회 일정표를 보고 대화를 완성하시오.

20th School Art Festival

October 4 (Fri.)

Event	Time (p.m.)	Place
play	2:00 – 3:00	Main Hall
magic show	3:00 – 4:00	Main Hall
concert	4:30 – 6:00	Gym

12
A: Where is the play?
B: It is _____.

13
A: When does the magic show begin?
B: It _____.

14
A: What time is the concert?
B: It is _____ 4:30 p.m. _____ 6 p.m.

15 다음 중 어법상 옳은 것을 모두 고르시오.

① Matilda looked after my dog.
② It was my first visit to Spain.
③ My family ate out at Mother's Day.
④ They watched a movie in last night.
⑤ I fell asleep for the math class.

다음 빈칸에 들어갈 말을 바르게 짝지은 것을 고르시오.

16

> ⓐ His parents took the expressway _____ London.
> ⓑ I can't forget the last scene _____ the movie.
> ⓒ The train runs _____ New York to Boston.

	ⓐ	ⓑ	ⓒ
①	to	– on	– from
②	to	– of	– from
③	to	– of	– next
④	for	– on	– next
⑤	for	– on	– from

17

> ⓐ Be kind _____ others.
> ⓑ I was at the hospital _____ five days.
> ⓒ There's a new restaurant between 5th Street _____ 6th Street.

	ⓐ	ⓑ	ⓒ
①	on	– at	– to
②	on	– during	– and
③	to	– for	– but
④	to	– for	– and
⑤	to	– during	– and

서술형

[18-19] 우리말과 뜻이 같도록 문장을 완성하시오.

18 너와 네 여동생은 오전 7시와 8시 사이에 도착해야 한다.
→ You and your sister should arrive _____ 7 a.m. _____ 8 a.m.

19 나는 크리스마스트리 아래에 선물을 하나 놓았다.
→ I put a gift _____ the Christmas tree.

서술형 NEW 내신 기출

20 다음 글에서 어법상 틀린 부분이 있는 문장을 찾아 바르게 고쳐 다시 쓰시오.

> ⓐ It was snowing outside. ⓑ Emily was looking out the window. ⓒ Jason was listening at music. ⓓ Their cat was sleeping under the table. ⓔ They had a peaceful time at home.

→ _____

서술형

21 다음 대화의 빈칸에 알맞은 전치사를 쓰시오.

Jake: I'm going to play baseball _____ my friends _____ Sunday.
Clark: Really? Can I join you?
Jake: Sure. Let's meet _____ the park _____ four o'clock.
Clark: Okay. See you then.

서술형 고난도

22 다음 광고에서 어법상 틀린 것을 모두 골라 바르게 고치시오.

> ***Grand Opening Sale!***
> We have everything from pens ① and diaries. All items are 50% off ② during the event. Our shop is ③ next to Sky Dentist. We open ④ on 8 a.m. Come by! We'll be waiting for you ⑤ at the store.

CHAPTER

13

접속사

and, but, or, so

○ 접속사 and, but, or, so는 문법적으로 대등한 역할을 하는 단어와 단어, 구와 구, 또는 절과 절을 이어 준다.

1 and: '그리고'
I will bring *a hat* **and** *sunscreen*.
Why don't you *sit down* **and** *rest* for a while?
I wrote Jake a letter, **and** *he liked it*.

> **both A and B**: 'A와 B 모두[둘 다]'
> I like **both** *pizza* **and** *pasta*.
> **Both** *Anthony* **and** *I* are middle school students.

2 but: '그러나', '그런데'
I can remember *her face* **but** not *her name*.
Chloe did her best, **but** *she didn't pass the test*.

3 or: '…나', '또는'
Which do you like better, *summer* **or** *winter*?
Are you *leaving home* **or** *coming home*?

> **either A or B**: 'A이거나 B이거나'
> Call me **either** *today* **or** *tomorrow*.
> You can **either** *stay here* **or** *follow me inside*.

4 so: '그래서'
He didn't have enough money, **so** *he had to go home*.
It was very cold, **so** *I closed the window*.

SPEED CHECK

( ) 안에서 알맞은 말을 고르시오.

1 They got married (and / or) lived a happy life.

2 I ate dinner, (or / but) now I'm hungry again.

3 I want to join either the tennis club (or / but) the painting club.

4 I suddenly felt sick, (so / but) I went to see a doctor immediately.

5 Which do you want, chicken (but / or) beef?

6 Laughing is good for both your mind (and / but) body.

PRACTICE TEST

정답 및 해설 p.33

A 두 문장의 뜻이 같도록 빈칸에 알맞은 접속사를 쓰시오.

1 You may go there. You may stay here.
→ You may go there _____ stay here.

2 This car doesn't look good. It is very safe.
→ This car doesn't look good, _____ it is very safe.

3 Leonardo da Vinci was a great artist. He was a great scientist too.
→ Leonardo da Vinci was a great artist _____ scientist.

A
safe 형 안전한
artist 명 예술가

B 다음 빈칸에 문맥상 알맞은 접속사를 쓰시오.

1 New York _____ Chicago are in the USA.
2 Which size do you want, regular _____ large?
3 I like _____ Japanese food _____ Italian food.
4 Roy invited Kate _____ Nick to the party, _____ they didn't come.
5 I ordered an iced coffee, _____ I received a hot one.
6 We can _____ stay at home _____ go to the park now.
7 Jason lies a lot, _____ I don't trust him.

B
regular 형 규칙적인;
*(크기가) 보통의
invite 동 초대하다
receive 동 받다
trust 동 믿다

C 우리말과 뜻이 같도록 주어진 말을 사용하여 문장을 완성하시오.

1 나의 고향은 아름답고 평화롭다. (beautiful, peaceful)
My hometown is _____ _____ _____.

2 이 신발은 싸지만 편하다. (cheap, comfortable)
These shoes are _____ _____ _____.

3 우리는 프랑스와 스페인을 둘 다 방문했다. (France, Spain)
We visited _____ _____ _____ _____.

4 내가 기타를 하나 갖고 있어서 너에게 그것을 빌려줄 수 있어. (lend)
I have a guitar, _____ _____ _____ _____ _____ to you.

5 너는 학교에 버스를 타고 가니, 지하철을 타고 가니? (by bus, by subway)
Do you go to school _____ _____ _____ _____ _____?

C
peaceful 형 평화로운
cheap 형 값이 싼
comfortable 형 편한
lend 동 빌려주다
subway 명 지하철

when, before, after, while

○ 시간을 나타내는 접속사 when, before, after, while 등은 절과 절을 이어 주는 접속사로, 접속사가 포함된 절이 다른 절의 내용을 보충한다.

1 when: '…할 때'

When Noah arrived home, he was very tired.
Cross the street **when** the light is green.

2 before: '…하기 전에'

I asked a question **before** the class ended.
Before you go outside, put your jacket on.

3 after: '…한 후에'

I remembered the answer **after** I read the hint.
After they won the game, they had a party.

4 while: '…하는 동안에'

While they watched a movie, they had some popcorn.
Stella was listening to music **while** she read a magazine.

> **Tip 주의!** 시간을 나타내는 접속사가 이끄는 절에서는 미래를 나타내더라도 미래시제 대신 현재시제를 쓴다.
> *After* Mandy **walks** her dog, she will bathe it.
> (← *After* Mandy **will walk** her dog, she will bathe it.)

 Grammar UP 접속사 when과 의문사 when의 구별

1 접속사 when('…할 때'): 『when+주어+동사』

When *you need* my help, please let me know.

2 의문사 when('언제'): 『When+동사+주어 ...?』

When *is your birthday*?

SPEED CHECK

우리말과 뜻이 같도록 (   ) 안에서 알맞은 말을 고르시오.

1 우리는 말하기 전에 생각해야 한다.

We should think (before / after) we speak.

2 너는 외국에 갈 때 네 여권을 가져가야 한다.

You have to bring your passport (after / when) you go abroad.

3 그녀는 저 시트콤을 보고 난 후 Adam의 팬이 되었다.

(After / When) she watched that sitcom, she became a fan of Adam.

4 나의 아내가 빨래하고 있는 동안에 나는 설거지를 했다.

(While / Before) my wife was doing laundry, I washed the dishes.

PRACTICE TEST

정답 및 해설 p.33

A 우리말과 뜻이 같도록 빈칸에 알맞은 접속사를 쓰시오.

1 Emily는 그녀의 옷을 갈아입은 후에 체육관에 갔다.

Emily went to the gym _____ she changed her clothes.

2 그는 공부하기 전에 자주 커피를 마신다.

He often drinks coffee _____ he studies.

3 TV를 켰을 때 나는 내가 가장 좋아하는 가수를 보았다.

_____ I turned on the TV, I saw my favorite singer.

4 우리는 그를 기다리는 동안에 우리의 현장 학습에 관해 얘기했다.

_____ we waited for him, we talked about our field trip.

A
gym ⑲ 체육관
change one's clothes
옷을 갈아입다
field trip 현장 학습

B 보기에서 알맞은 말을 골라 문장을 완성하시오.

보기	when I was in Italy	after I take a shower
	while I was sleeping	before I went to bed

1 I will call you _____.

2 My mom used to read me stories _____.

3 I worked for a trading company _____.

4 The thief stole my bag _____.

B
take a shower 샤워하다
trading company
무역 회사
steal ⑧ 훔치다
(steal-stole)

C 우리말과 뜻이 같도록 주어진 말을 사용하여 문장을 완성하시오.

1 너는 저녁을 먹기 전에 손을 씻어야 한다. (have dinner)

_____ _____ _____ _____, you should wash your hands.

2 내가 거리를 걷고 있는 동안에 나는 나의 선생님을 만났다. (walk)

_____ _____ _____ _____ down the street, I met my teacher.

3 너는 물을 끓인 후에 달걀을 냄비에 넣어라. (boil, the water)

_____ _____ _____ _____ _____, put the eggs into the pot.

4 이 앱을 업데이트할 때 나는 와이파이를 사용할 것이다. (update)

I will use WiFi _____ _____ _____ this app.

C
walk down the street
길을 걷다
boil ⑧ 끓이다
pot ⑲ 냄비
update ⑧ 갱신하다,
…을 최신식으로 하다
app ⑲ 앱, 응용 프로그램

because, if, that

○ 접속사 because, if, that은 절과 절을 이어 주는 접속사로, 접속사가 포함된 절이 다른 절의 내용을 보충한다.

1 because: '… 때문에' (원인, 이유)

Robert goes to the gym **because** the trainer is helpful.

I took a taxi **because** I missed the last bus.

2 if: '만약 …라면' (조건)

If I have free time, I'll read a book.

If you meet her, you'll like her.

> **Tip 주의!** 조건의 접속사가 이끄는 절에서는 미래를 나타내더라도 미래시제 대신 현재시제를 쓴다.
>
> *If* you **go** to the party this weekend, you will see him.
>
> (← *If* you **will go** to the party this weekend, you will see him.)

3 that: '…인 것', '…하는 것'

• 주어, 목적어, 보어로 쓰이는 명사절을 이끈다.

• that절을 목적어로 취하는 동사: think, believe, hope, tell, say, know 등

1) **주어**: '…하는 것은'

That he is late is not surprising.

→ **It** is not surprising **that** he is late.

> **Tip 주의!** that절이 주어로 쓰일 경우, 『it(가주어) … that(진주어)』으로 쓰는 것이 더 일반적이다.

2) **목적어**: '…하는 것을' (that 생략 가능)

I hope (**that**) you will get better soon.

3) **보어**: '…하는 것(이다)'

The bad news is **that** there was a car accident.

> **Grammar UP** that의 여러 가지 쓰임
>
> **1** 명사절을 이끄는 that: She said **that** she loved him.
>
> **2** '저것'의 뜻인 that: **That** is my favorite food.
>
> **3** '저 …'의 뜻으로, 명사를 꾸며주는 that: **That** movie is interesting.

SPEED CHECK

빈칸에 알맞은 말을 고르시오.

1 I turned off the TV _____ the show was boring.

① before   ② that   ③ because   ④ but   ⑤ or

2 _____ we take the subway, we can be there in an hour.

① If   ② That   ③ Before   ④ But   ⑤ And

PRACTICE TEST

정답 및 해설 p.34

A ( ) 안에서 알맞은 말을 고르시오.

1 (That / If) it snows tomorrow, we will build a snowman.
2 I took extra classes (that / because) I'm not good at math.
3 Most people knew (that / because) the story was true.
4 (Because / If) Justin is very nice, everyone likes him.

A
build ⑧ 짓다; *만들다
snowman ⑲ 눈사람
extra ⑲ 추가의
be good at …을 잘하다

B 내용이 자연스럽게 이어지도록 문장을 연결하시오.

1 We believe •   • ⓐ because I came home late.
2 If we can't get tickets, •   • ⓑ we will stay home.
3 My mom got angry •   • ⓒ that this movie will be a big hit.

B
big hit 대히트, 대성공

C 다음 문장에서 <u>틀린</u> 부분을 찾아 바르게 고치시오.

1 It is important if we finish on time.
2 The team won if they had a good coach.
3 His problem is because he is too lazy.
4 That you have a dream, do your best to achieve it.

C
on time
시간을 어기지 않고, 정각에
coach ⑲ (경기 등의) 코치
lazy ⑲ 게으른
do one's best
최선을 다하다
achieve ⑧ 성취하다

D 우리말과 뜻이 같도록 주어진 말을 사용하여 문장을 완성하시오.

1 나는 네가 내일 그 시험에 합격하기를 바란다. (will pass)
I hope _____ _____ _____ _____ the exam tomorrow.

2 Emma는 아무것도 먹지 않았기 때문에 어지러움을 느꼈다. (eat anything)
Emma felt dizzy _____ _____ _____ _____ _____.

3 만약 네가 내일 한가하면 함께 쇼핑하러 가자. (free)
_____ _____ _____ _____ tomorrow, let's go shopping together.

4 그가 네 가지 언어를 말할 수 있는 것은 놀랍다. (can speak)
It is amazing _____ _____ _____ _____ four languages.

D
pass ⑧ 지나가다; *합격하다
dizzy ⑲ 어지러운
free ⑲ 자유로운; 한가한
language ⑲ 언어

REVIEW TEST

[01-02] 다음 빈칸에 들어갈 수 있는 말을 고르시오.

01

> Which do you want to eat, bread _____ rice?

① and　　　　② but
③ or　　　　　④ so
⑤ that

02

> _____ Clara was young, she hoped to be a doctor.

① Before　　　② After
③ If　　　　　④ That
⑤ When

NEW 내신 기출
03 다음 우리말을 영어로 옮겨 쓸 때 사용되지 <u>않는</u> 표현은?

> Ann은 재즈를 좋아하지만 그녀의 여동생은 좋아하지 않는다.

① so　　　　　② her
③ sister　　　 ④ likes
⑤ doesn't

서술형
[04-07] 보기에서 알맞은 접속사를 골라 빈칸에 쓰시오.

보기
before　　before　　if　　when

04 Don't forget to brush your teeth _____ you go to sleep.

05 I will be very happy _____ I meet my favorite movie star.

06 I like spring best _____ there are many flowers.

07 Sally's hair was longer _____ she was a student.

[08-09] 다음 빈칸에 공통으로 들어갈 수 있는 말을 고르시오.

08

> • June wanted sandwich for lunch, _____ I wanted steak.
> • My parents don't like hip-hop, _____ I do.

① and　　　　② because
③ but　　　　 ④ after
⑤ or

09

> • Everyone thinks _____ he is an honest man.
> • Who is _____ boy over there?

① and　　　　② that
③ when　　　 ④ before
⑤ because

132

10 주어진 문장과 같은 뜻이 되도록 조건에 맞게 문장을 완성하시오.

> She cleaned the house and then cooked dinner.
> → _____
> → _____

> ───────| 조건 |───────
> • 시간을 나타내는 접속사 2개를 각 문장에 한 번씩 사용할 것
> • 시간을 나타내는 접속사가 문두에 오도록 쓸 것
> • 8단어의 완전한 문장으로 쓸 것

[13-14] 다음 중 <u>어색한</u> 문장을 고르시오.

13 ① Make a reservation before you visit the restaurant.
② If Ms. Johnson is late, let's start without her.
③ Because the dress didn't fit, I didn't buy it.
④ I'd like to visit the Eiffel Tower and the Louvre.
⑤ After the food goes bad, put it in the refrigerator.

[11-12] 다음 빈칸에 들어갈 말을 바르게 짝지은 것을 고르시오.

11
> ⓐ Sam _____ John are my classmates.
> ⓑ I cleaned my room _____ my mom went to the market.

	ⓐ	ⓑ		ⓐ	ⓑ
①	and	– while	②	or	– before
③	but	– or	④	and	– or
⑤	or	– while			

14 ① After he missed the bus, he ran to school.
② We can take either a bus but a taxi.
③ If you are hungry, I will make you something to eat.
④ It is strange that Anna is so angry all the time.
⑤ Jamie broke his arm while he was playing basketball.

12
> ⓐ _____ Emily doesn't pass the audition, she won't become a singer.
> ⓑ I believe _____ she will make the right choice.

	ⓐ	ⓑ		ⓐ	ⓑ
①	Because	– after	②	When	– that
③	If	– after	④	When	– if
⑤	If	– that			

15 다음 대화의 빈칸에 알맞은 접속사를 쓰시오.

A: You don't look good. What's wrong?
B: I'm worried _____ my cat is missing.
A: That's too bad. I hope _____ she will come back soon.

[16-17] 다음 두 문장을 보기와 같이 바꿔 쓰시오.

| 보기 |

The ice is melting. That is true.
→ It is true that the ice is melting.

16 We'll go to Hawaii on vacation. That is wonderful.

→ _____

_____ on vacation.

17 He gave his mother flowers. That was touching.

→ _____

_____

[18-20] 주어진 말을 사용하여 두 문장을 한 문장으로 만드시오.

18 Mark ate too many apples. He got sick.

(before)

→ Mark ate too many apples _____

_____ .

19 James likes math. He likes science too.

(both)

→ James likes _____ .

20 Emily is thirsty. She wants some water.

(because)

→ Emily wants some water _____

_____ .

21 다음 광고를 보고 대화를 완성하시오.

Roberto's Pizzeria

· Delivery in 30 minutes
  (If we're late, it's free.)
· All kinds of pizzas
· Sizes: small / medium / large

Ryan: I'm hungry. Let's order a pizza.
Anna: Good idea. Look! _____ _____
   _____ get our pizza in 30 minutes,
   it's free!
Ryan: Great! Which size do you want—small,
   medium, _____ large?
Anna: How about large?
Ryan: Sure.

22 다음 중 어법상 옳은 것은 모두 몇 개인가?

ⓐ It was amazing that John saved a girl.
ⓑ If you'll try the pie, you'll buy it.
ⓒ People got on the train after arrived.
ⓓ Elizabeth woke up because she heard a
  strange sound.
ⓔ Please bring both your swimsuit and
  swimming cap.

① 1개　　② 2개　　③ 3개
④ 4개　　⑤ 5개

[01-04] 다음 빈칸에 들어갈 수 있는 말을 고르시오.

01

| He _____ out two hours ago. |

① go   ② is going
③ goes   ④ went
⑤ will go

02

| Chloe can go fishing tomorrow, _____? |

① isn't she   ② doesn't she
③ shouldn't she   ④ can't she
⑤ won't she

03

| _____ shopping is very fun. |

① Go   ② Going
③ To going   ④ Goes
⑤ Went

04

| Take an umbrella, _____ you will get wet. |

① if   ② or
③ so   ④ and
⑤ but

05 다음 중 어법상 <u>틀린</u> 것은?

① You are kind.
② We are very hungry.
③ The children is happy.
④ They are good friends.
⑤ Mr. Kent is very handsome.

NEW **내신 기출**

06 다음 빈칸에 들어갈 수 있는 것을 모두 고르면?

| I _____ working on the project. |

① hoped   ② enjoyed
③ wanted   ④ finished
⑤ decided

07 우리말과 뜻이 같도록 할 때 빈칸에 들어갈 수 있는 것은?

| 너는 걱정할 필요가 없다.
→ You _____ worry. |

① can't   ② must not
③ don't have to   ④ may not
⑤ will not

서술형 **NEW** **내신 기출**

08 다음 대화의 주어진 말을 바르게 배열하여 문장을 완성하고 해석하시오.

| A: Would you like something to drink?
B: Yes. (water, a, I, of, want, glass). |

→ _____

→ _____

09 보기의 밑줄 친 <u>must</u>와 뜻이 같은 것은?

| 보기 |
> He <u>must</u> be very tired now.

① She <u>must</u> be his aunt.

② <u>Must</u> I take him there?

③ You <u>must</u> not swim here.

④ You <u>must</u> go to bed now.

⑤ We <u>must</u> be quiet in the library.

10 다음 밑줄 친 부분과 바꿔 쓸 수 있는 것은?

> Jenny <u>was not able to</u> find her backpack.

① didn't have to   ② may not

③ must not   ④ shouldn't

⑤ couldn't

11 다음 중 어법상 옳은 것은?

① It's not expensive, isn't it?

② He knows you, doesn't he?

③ You don't like sports, don't you?

④ You went to the movies, don't you?

⑤ Tom doesn't like science, does Tom?

[12-13] 우리말과 뜻이 같도록 주어진 말을 사용하여 문장을 완성하시오.

12 우리는 휴가를 어디로 갈 것인지에 대해 이야기했다. (go)

→ We talked about _____ _____ _____
   on a vacation.

13 나는 그 고양이가 상자 안에서 놀고 있는 것을 보았다.
(see, the cat, play)

→ I _____ _____ _____ _____ in the
   box.

14 보기의 밑줄 친 부분과 쓰임이 같은 것은?

| 보기 |
> We need some bread <u>to eat</u>.

① He grew up <u>to be</u> a scientist.

② My hope is <u>to see</u> him again.

③ Give me a good book <u>to read</u>.

④ The doctor decided <u>to take</u> X-rays.

⑤ I went to the market <u>to buy</u> some food.

[15-17] 보기에서 알맞은 말을 골라 대화를 완성하시오.

| 보기 |
> or   and   but   because

15 A: Which do you like more, comedies _____
     romance movies?

   B: I like comedies.

16 A: What's your favorite season?

   B: I love winter most _____ I can build
     snowmen.

17 A: What do you think about this red sweater?

B: Well, it's beautiful, _____ it's too small for me.

20

A: What time do you get up ___ⓐ___ Sundays?

B: ___ⓑ___ nine a.m.

	ⓐ	ⓑ			ⓐ	ⓑ
①	on	In		②	at	In
③	on	At		④	on	On
⑤	at	On				

18 다음 빈칸에 공통으로 들어갈 수 있는 것은?

> • Both Mary _____ Jane were late for school.
> • Leave now, _____ you'll be in time for the movie.

① and   ② but

③ or   ④ because

⑤ so

서술형

21 다음 대화의 빈칸에 알맞은 말을 쓰시오.

Amy: I'm hungry. Do you have _____ food?

Paul: I have _____ chocolate. Would you like one?

Amy: Sure. Thanks.

서술형

[22-24] 다음 중학생들이 선호하는 여가 활동에 대한 표를 보고, 주어진 말을 사용하여 문장을 완성하시오.

Activity	surf the Internet	watch TV	play games
Percent	30%	40%	30%

22 Watching TV is _____ _____ than playing games. (popular)

[19-20] 다음 대화의 빈칸에 들어갈 말을 바르게 짝지은 것을 고르시오.

19

A: ___ⓐ___ is that man?

B: He is Mr. Brown.

A: ___ⓑ___ does he do for a living?

B: He is an engineer.

23 Watching TV is _____ _____ _____ activity among students. (popular)

	ⓐ	ⓑ			ⓐ	ⓑ
①	How	What		②	Who	What
③	What	What		④	Who	How
⑤	Who	When				

24 Surfing the Internet is _____ _____ _____ playing games. (popular)

[01-02] 다음 빈칸에 들어갈 수 있는 말을 고르시오.

01

> Will he _____ back tomorrow morning?

① be   ② is

③ are   ④ was

⑤ were

02

> My brother needed a lot of money _____ Sydney.

① visit   ② to visiting

③ visited   ④ visits

⑤ to visit

[03-04] 다음 빈칸에 들어갈 수 <u>없는</u> 말을 고르시오.

03

> There are _____ tall buildings in this city.

① ten   ② much

③ many   ④ some

⑤ lots of

04

> Daniel played tennis _____.

① last night   ② yesterday

③ tomorrow   ④ this morning

⑤ last weekend

서술형 **NEW** **내신 기출**

05 우리말과 뜻이 같도록 주어진 철자로 시작하여 문장을 완성하시오.

우리는 너에게 무엇을 할지 말해 줄 거야.

→ W_____ w_____ t_____ y_____
w_____ t_____ d_____.

06 보기의 밑줄 친 cannot과 의미가 같은 것은?

| 보기 |
> She <u>cannot</u> be hungry already.

① You <u>cannot</u> park here.

② I <u>cannot</u> speak French.

③ She <u>cannot</u> find her keys.

④ Ms. Lee <u>cannot</u> be in the school now.

⑤ He <u>cannot</u> finish the homework by then.

서술형

07 두 문장의 뜻이 같도록 빈칸에 알맞은 말을 쓰시오.

Jane got up so early that she could go jogging.
→ Jane got up early _____ to go jogging.

08 다음 밑줄 친 that의 쓰임이 나머지와 <u>다른</u> 것은?

① She said <u>that</u> it was not hers.

② I don't want to read <u>that</u> book.

③ I thought <u>that</u> he was very brave.

④ The truth is <u>that</u> the man is a thief.

⑤ It is surprising <u>that</u> she came back so early.

서술형

[09-12] 다음 문장에서 <u>틀린</u> 부분을 찾아 바르게 고치시오.

09 The girl looks very beautifully.

(   ) → (   )

10 He had few money, so he couldn't buy it.

(   ) → (   )

11 They were very busy to make plans for the vacation.

(   ) → (   )

12 This room is so small to hold five people.

(   ) → (   )

[13-14] 다음 중 어법상 <u>틀린</u> 것을 고르시오.

13 ① I have some good news.

② Did you bring any snacks?

③ I don't have some pens with me.

④ Some people think that he was right.

⑤ She doesn't have any books at home.

14 ① Is it true that he will marry Emily?

② He learned how to play the piano.

③ She left early because she had something to do.

④ Clean your room right now, and you can go out with Frank.

⑤ Before she went to sleep, Kate finished to do her homework.

서술형

15 다음 빈칸에 공통으로 들어갈 수 있는 말을 쓰시오.

• _____ is 4 a.m. now.

• _____ is Monday today.

[16-17] 다음 중 어법상 <u>틀린</u> 것을 고르시오.

16 I ① usually get up ② at 7 a.m. ③ at the morning. I ④ have to get ⑤ to school by 8:30.

17 I heard that ① he cut oneself. It ② was really surprising ③ because he ④ always looked very ⑤ cautious.

서술형

[18-20] 우리말과 뜻이 같도록 주어진 말을 바르게 배열하시오.

18 우리 어머니는 내가 낫게 하기 위해 내게 수프를 조금 주셨다.

(feel, make, to, better, me)

→ My mother gave me some soup _____

_____.

19 걱정하지 마. 그는 네게 그 책을 가져다줄 수 있을 거야.

(be, to, able, will, bring)

→ Don't worry. He _____

_____ you the book.

20 정말 흥미진진한 영화였어!

(it, exciting, an, movie, what, was)

→ _____!

21 보기의 단어로 빈칸을 완성할 수 <u>없는</u> 것은?

| 보기 |
How   Why   Who   When   What

① A: _____ do you like soccer?

B: Because it is very fun.

② A: _____ does your aunt do?

B: She is an animal trainer.

③ A: _____ is your favorite writer?

B: Ernest Hemingway.

④ A: _____ is the nearest bakery?

B: It's next to the supermarket.

⑤ A: _____ do you take ballet lessons?

B: On Tuesdays and Fridays.

[22-24] 다음 빈칸에 들어갈 말을 바르게 짝지은 것을 고르시오.

22

She had three cars. I still remember the silver ⓐ . ⓑ was really cool.

	ⓐ	ⓑ		ⓐ	ⓑ
①	one	– One	②	one	– It
③	it	– It	④	it	– That
⑤	that	– It			

23

ⓐ Ann's husband gave a diamond ring _____ her.

ⓑ _____ make sandwiches for lunch, I bought some bread.

	ⓐ	ⓑ		ⓐ	ⓑ
①	to	– To	②	for	– Of
③	to	– Of	④	on	– For
⑤	to	– On			

24

Nora: Take a look at this dress.

Henry: ⓐ beautiful!

Nora: I'll wear it to the party on Friday night. ⓑ do you think?

Henry: I'm sure that you will look wonderful.

	ⓐ	ⓑ		ⓐ	ⓑ
①	How	– What	②	What	– Why
③	How	– Why	④	What	– What
⑤	How	– Who			

[25-26] 우리말과 뜻이 같도록 주어진 말을 사용하여 문장을 완성하시오.

25 나는 절대 학교에 지각하지 않는다. (be late for)

→ I _____ .

26 너는 언제나 나에게서 책들을 빌릴 수 있다. (borrow)

→ _____ _____ _____ _____ _____

from me.

불규칙 동사표

현재	과거	뜻
am, is / are	was / were	…이다; 있다
become	became	되다
begin	began	시작하다
bite	bit	물다
blow	blew	불다
break	broke	깨다
bring	brought	가져오다
build	built	짓다
buy	bought	사다
catch	caught	잡다
choose	chose	선택하다
come	came	오다
cost	cost	(비용이 얼마) 들다
cut	cut	자르다
deal	dealt	다루다
dig	dug	(구덩이를) 파다
do	did	하다
draw	drew	당기다; 그리다
drink	drank	마시다
drive	drove	운전하다
eat	ate	먹다
fall	fell	떨어지다
feed	fed	먹이다
feel	felt	느끼다
fight	fought	싸우다
find	found	찾다
fly	flew	날다
forget	forgot	잊어버리다
forgive	forgave	용서하다
get	got	받다; 얻다
give	gave	주다
go	went	가다
grow	grew	자라다; 기르다
have	had	가지고 있다
hear	heard	듣다
hide	hid	숨다
hold	held	(손에) 들다, 쥐다
hurt	hurt	다치게 하다; 아프다
keep	kept	보유하다; 지키다
know	knew	알다
lay	laid	놓다
lead	led	이끌다

현재	과거	뜻
leave	left	떠나다
lend	lent	빌려주다
let	let	시키다
lie	lay	눕다
lose	lost	잃다
make	made	만들다
mean	meant	의미하다
meet	met	만나다
pay	paid	지불하다
put	put	놓다
quit	quit	그만두다
read	read	읽다
ride	rode	(탈것을) 타다
ring	rang	전화하다; 울리다
rise	rose	오르다, 솟아오르다
run	ran	달리다
say	said	(…라고) 말하다
see	saw	보다
seek	sought	찾다; (충고 등을) 구하다
sell	sold	팔다
send	sent	보내다
set	set	놓다; 배치하다
shake	shook	흔들다; 흔들리다
shine	shone	빛나다
sing	sang	노래하다
sink	sank	가라앉다
sit	sat	앉다
sleep	slept	자다
speak	spoke	말하다
spend	spent	(돈·시간 등을) 쓰다
stand	stood	서 있다
steal	stole	훔치다
swim	swam	수영하다
take	took	가지고 가다; 취하다
teach	taught	가르치다
tell	told	말하다
think	thought	생각하다
throw	threw	던지다
understand	understood	이해하다
wake	woke	깨우다
wear	wore	입고 있다
win	won	이기다
write	wrote	쓰다

지은이

NE능률 영어교육연구소

NE능률 영어교육연구소는 혁신적이며 효율적인 영어 교재를 개발하고
영어 학습의 질을 한 단계 높이고자 노력하는 NE능률의 연구조직입니다.

1316 GRAMMAR 〈LEVEL 1〉

펴낸이	주민홍
펴낸곳	서울특별시 마포구 월드컵북로 396(상암동) 누리꿈스퀘어 비즈니스타워 10층
	(주)NE능률 (우편번호 03925)
펴낸날	2024년 1월 5일 개정판 제1쇄 발행
	2024년 2월 15일 제2쇄
전화	02 2014 7114
팩스	02 3142 0356
홈페이지	www.neungyule.com
등록번호	제 1-68호
ISBN	979-11-253-4284-7
정가	14,500원

NE 능률

고객센터

교재 내용 문의 : contact.nebooks.co.kr (별도의 가입 절차 없이 작성 가능)
제품 구매, 교환, 불량, 반품 문의 : 02-2014-7114
☎ 전화문의는 본사 업무시간 중에만 가능합니다.